SHOOT FOR THE STARS AND YOU WILL LAND ON THE MOON

ABOUT THE AUTHOR

Leopoldo Fernández Pujals is the founder of Telepizza and until its recent sale to Orange, was the Chairman and principal shareholder of Jazztel. Cuban by birth, Mr. Fernandez Pujals went into exile with his family in the United States after the rise of Fidel Castro. He joined the U.S. Army and participated in the Vietnam War. Later, he graduated with degrees in Accounting and Finance from Stetson University. He began working at Procter & Gamble and then at Johnson & Johnson, the company that brought him to Spain in 1981. In 1987, he opened his first pizzeria offering home delivery in Spain. After the sale of TelePizza in 1999, when the company had 800 stores, Mr. Fernandez commenced another business endeavor, this time in the telecommunications sector. He became the principle shareholder of Jazztel, rescuing the company from insolvency and then growing the business into the Ibex 35 despite fierce competition from incumbent giants.

Mr. Fernández Pujals is currently working on several new projects, both business and philanthropical, including horse breeder Yeguada Centurión, which arises from his desire to improve the horse of the pure Spanish breed.

Mr. Fernández Pujals is married, has five sons and three grandchildren.

Leopoldo Fernández Pujals

SHOOT FOR THE STARS AND YOU WILL LAND ON THE MOON

TURN YOUR
DREAMS INTO REALITY

C

TABLE OF CONTENTS

Acknowledgents

I would like to express my gratitude to:

- My wife, Marilina, who not only wrote the prologue of this book but has loved and supported me during the wonderful years that we have been together.

- My children, for the unconditional love they have given to me. I hope this book will help them to remain united and continue our family legacy.

- Perico Español, who, for almost 30 years, has remained a loyal, dedicated friend and business partner, and who spent hours helping me with this book.

- Raúl Rivero, for writing the epilogue and for putting on the final, poetic touch and giving a deep sense of patriotism to this book.

- Each and every person who shared their testimonies with affection and respect.

- You, the reader. I hope the content and message of this book will inspire you to fulfill your dreams.

LEOPOLDO FERNÁNDEZ PUJALS

PROLOGUE

BY MARILINA VÍLCHEZ JORDÁN

I met my husband, Leopoldo (Leo, as he likes to be called), in the summer of 1990 through an ad in the newspaper. I was a post-graduate student in Human Resources at the Universidad Pontificia de Comillas. Like most eager graduate students, I spent every Sunday scanning the classified advertisements looking for job opportunities. The previous year I had completed my degree at the University of Granada in psychology. My objective was to professionally apply what I had learned during the course of my college career as a Human Resources executive in the private sector.

The ad that appeared in the newspaper that fateful Sunday was very generic. It did not list the name of the company or the position available. The ad was written in a manner to entice young college graduates to begin their professional careers in a fast-growing company. It turned out that they were looking for future store manager trainees for TelePizza, a dynamic pizza company with 13 company-owned and franchised stores.

The company was not known to the public at the time. They must have set my resume aside in a special box, because I did not hear from them right away. I eventually received a callback when they decided to create a Human Resources department.

When I answered the telephone, the voice on the other end was persuasive, deep but softened by an accent that could have been from the Canary Islands. He introduced himself as Leopoldo Fernández Pujals, President of TelePizza. We set the date, time, and place for the interview. The company's main office was located in Madrid on Pío XII Street in a 2,500-square-foot space. The interview took place in a small room with two desks. At one of them sat Leopoldo. As he stood up to greet me I noticed his appearance. He wore the uniform of all TelePizza store employees: a white polo shirt with the TelePizza logo, blue jeans and topsiders nautical shoes, which he wore without any socks, even during winter. He had a red baseball cap attached to his belt.

My first impression was that a peculiar, different, and very original individual was in front of me. I had just finished doing a number of job interviews. I was still awaiting replies from various companies, and in every one of those interviews, the Human Resources directors, and in some cases even the President, had shown up impeccably dressed in a suit and tie. Of course, this was considered the norm in the business world. Soon I would learn that a true entrepreneur is genuine, different from the rest, a mold breaker, both in the way they think as well as in their behavior and attitude.

His relaxed demeanor was not the only attribute that intrigued me about him. He was one of those people who was naturally warm and friendly but, at the same time, commanded respect. When the interview started I noticed that he had incredible enthusiasm, which was reflected in his eyes and even in the way he gestured with his hands. He explained to me TelePizza's plans for expansion. As he spoke I was persuaded that the 13 stores that already existed would multiply in a few years and become 200 throughout Spain. There was no doubt in his tone of voice. He was a dreamer and a visionary. As a Human Resources professional, the project and the job sounded extremely attractive to me. Leo had sold me on the project to the point that I became enthused about the challenge ahead.

During the course of the interview, he asked me two questions that I will never forget, and I eventually incorporated them in my own interviews during my tenure with the company. The first, to define myself in one word, was not that difficult. The second question caught me by surprise, but I responded sincerely without any excuses.

Leo: "Are you good with numbers?"

Me: "No."

Leo: "What is the product of 13 times 13?" he asked anyway, staring straight into my eyes.

Me: "I have already told you that I am not good with numbers. I am a right-brained creative person."

I said this without even trying to formulate the correct answer in my mind, using "usted", which is the way to formally respond in a professional manner in Spanish.

Leo did not bat an eye that I did not answer the question, because I had been direct and honest. Instead, he simply explained how to break down the simple math problem in one's head. This revealed another one of Leo's remarkable characteristics, his generosity. He enjoys sharing his knowledge, being a teacher. He has an amazing ability with numbers.

I should add that his demeanor was unpretentious, since he did not make me feel inferior for my lack of numerical ability. At the end of the interview, he summarized our conversation and asserted that TelePizza and I were made for each other. When I left the Pío XII Street office, I had no idea that I had just met my boss for the next three years, let alone my future husband and father of our three children.

My first months at TelePizza were hectic, to say the least. It was a young, dynamic growth company, in continual evolution. There were frenetic moments, since everything in the Human Resources department under my responsibility had to be resolved almost immediately. As there was not enough office space for all of us, I worked in the conference room, which I shared with the marketing director and Leo. When he arrived, I continued doing my interviews in the cafeteria, located on the bottom floor of the building.

Personnel recruitment took up most of my time, because it was urgent to fill all vacancies to comply with the growth plan and the mission of the company, "We Must Grow." I was not only involved in finding store managers with college degrees, but I also had to find the additional resources for the head office.

There was an unforgettable situation during my first month of employment. We had just finished defining the job profile of the pizza delivery person. We wanted to hire full-time college students who wished to work part time in order to make extra money for their personal expenses. I remember I hired a young man as a deliveryman, not because he fit the job description, but because I felt sorry for him. He led me to believe that he really needed the job in order to provide for his family. Well, a few weeks later, I was informed that he had left the job after stealing a considerable amount of money from his colleagues. It seems that the man was a drug addict. I felt ashamed for not performing my job correctly. When Leo found out, he was tolerant but firm with me. He sharply told me to learn from the experience, but that if I would rather do charity work, then I better go find another job at a convent assisting the nuns. And he was right.

After that I began feeling as if I was part of the enterprise and I concentrated on fulfilling my objectives in my area of responsibility. From this experience I learned that he was tolerant of mistakes made if they were done unintentionally. That is a characteristic of his that defines his business behavior. He believes that making mistakes is part of the learning process. Nevertheless, he does not accept people who behave maliciously. Initially he may appear naïve, offering many opportunities to people who do not deserve them, but he does not stutter when he needs to dismiss them. Firing bad employees at the right time is another trait of successful leaders.

I remember a year after I joined the company, we moved to a new building, doubling the size of our first offices. Leo met with me in my cubicle, which we called the fishbowl, because it was small and some of the walls were made of glass. When he left my office I counted 20 new jobs that needed to be filled at the head office, including a personnel director, a lawyer for the legal department, programmers for the information technology department, an auditor, a financial planner, a store construction manager, and other key positions. The task was so large that I had to hire another Human Resources specialist to assist me in the department.

I also recall that it was about this time that we hired Leo's first personal secretary. It was then that he had his first office with a desk. Up until then he met with visitors in the conference room. He would meet with other executives in their offices, or he would simply meet them at one of the pizza stores. At that time, TelePizza had a total of 40 stores. We all worked endless hours and were completely mesmerized by Leo's infectious vision. He was the first to arrive at the office and the last to leave. This is another one of his qualities: his energy. This last trait could become almost obsessive, since the entrepreneur does not stop until the project has been finalized or is well on its way to success.

Another area under my responsibility was personnel development, to which Leo gave great priority. We created the School of TelePizza Leadership. The initial course, based on Leo's business philosophy, was taught in the Gaztambide pizza store.

I really enjoyed the training programs. At the beginning, the store managers came to the job with very little leadership experience and minimal education. But every morning, before they opened their store, they participated in self-development courses. They were taught that "a leader can be created by learning the proper skills and acquiring the correct habits," and "the leader delegates tasks but does not disassociate himself from them."

We talked about enthusiasm, how to sell ideas, how to manage and motivate employees, and the difference between a constructive and a destructive mindset. We also taught the importance of a smile in every day dealings (especially with customers), how to dream big, the management cycle, that fear paralyzes you, that the antidote to fear is action, and so much more. The expression on the store managers' faces said everything. They were starting to believe in their leadership potential and they were grateful to TelePizza for investing in them. Every subject that was taught came from Leo's knowledge that he had acquired through reading dozens and dozens of self-development books throughout his life. From him I learned just about everything I know about this subject.

The Human Resources Department was responsible for many tasks, including writing every employee's job description, creating job performance evaluations, defining the appropriate salary range for each position, conducting annual salary reviews, etc. Additionally, there was everything else that people thought that Human Resources was responsible for.

Leo highly suggested that every office employee spend as many evenings as possible working at the pizza stores, as he did himself, leading by example. He explained to us that we had to better understand the business, and he often said that if we did not sell enough pizzas our jobs were not needed. It was clearly understood by everyone that the personnel working at the store were the most important, above all others, except for the customer, who was at the very top of the pyramid. This is another quality that stands out among entrepreneurs like him: they perform any task without feeling embarrassed, and no task is beneath their dignity. On the contrary, good, honest work that produces positive results is what motivates them. For example, Leo believes that sales courses should be taught at universities, when, in reality, most college graduates consider sales a second-tier position. He believes that knowing and practicing sales techniques are necessary not just professionally but in every facet of life. He says, with his Cuban accent, "My right arm is longer than my left," referring to the years he spent as a salesman with Johnson & Johnson carrying a heavy bag full of surgical instruments during his hospital visits.

I remember one of those evenings working at a pizza store making pizza, spreading tomato and cheese, and I will never forget the strong onion odor left on my hands for hours afterwards. When my mother came to visit me in Madrid, Leo insisted she come into the store, because he wanted to meet her. After meeting Leo, my mother, with her typical Andalusian accent, turned to me and said, "Watch out for this man, he likes you." Of course I thought my mother was imagining things.

In the days that followed I began to notice that Leo seemed happy whenever he saw me. This made me think that my mother's intuition was maybe right after all.

The sales abilities of an entrepreneur are above average, mainly because they are so convinced of the benefits of their product and that through their confidence and enthusiasm they are able to close the sale. They have no need for false pretenses. Simultaneously, they are specialists in finding out the needs of the customer. Being the entrepreneur that he is, Leo used all the sales techniques at his disposal to persuade me to marry him and become his wife. Without going into all the details, I can tell you that one day as we left a pizza store, he invited me to see the movie *Havana*. Afterward, we dined together. He displayed an enormous amount of self-confidence, stating directly, "You and I will marry and we will have many children." Since it was a statement and not a question, he did not receive a response from me. Of course, he previously had asked me what I wanted to do in the following five years, so he was aware that I wanted to get married and have a family.

We were married on June 9, 1992. Notwithstanding, I had him take the battery of tests at my disposal, intelligence and personality included, so that I would not have any unpleasant surprises. He passed all of them with flying colors. I was 25 years old and Leo was 45. He was my boss, divorced with children, and a Cuban. On the day of our wedding, my father-in-law, Genaro, who arrived from Fort Lauderdale accompanied by his second wife, Catherine, said, "My son is a very good person, noble and with a kind heart, but let me give you a piece of advice. When you want to reach the top of the mountain, I suggest that you circle around it to attain the pinnacle." He was paraphrasing the language of an entrepreneur: "Learn how to sell him the idea."

Up until that day Leo lived in an apartment that was virtually empty. It contained only two beds, the minimum amount of cutlery, and two chairs in which Alejandro and Carlos, Leo's sons from his first marriage, sat on to play their guitars. The chairs were collected by his children from a street dumpster during one of the summers that they were staying with him. I recall Carlos during his adolescent years asking me why his father was living in that manner. He was puzzled, because Leo had informed him of the profits that the business was producing, writing numbers down on a paper napkin. I had to explain to him that his father was reinvesting everything into the business, as he was concerned that "the giants, the Domino's and Pizza Huts, would eat him alive." The aim of an entrepreneur is not to acquire money but to make their dreams a reality. Money is only the financial resource that facilitates starting projects with new ideas. It is needed in all fast-growing businesses, but when the glass is more than half full, they contribute generously back to society through philanthropic endeavors.

I continued to work at TelePizza until shortly before the birth of our oldest son, Alberto. Leo actually fired me from the company when he instituted a new policy that direct relatives were not allowed to work together. At the time he imposed this rule, we were the only ones that did not comply with that rule. In the long run I approved of his decision, as we were about to embark on a new personal project raising our children. Additionally, I had lost the trust of most employees at TelePizza after they learned that the person heading the Human Resources department was Leo's wife. My professional life at TelePizza had reached a conclusion. I was happy to start our new project, which pleased me enormously, creating a family and providing the support an entrepreneur needs.

Leo and I have been through a lot together, and every experience just proves how strong he is. Entrepreneurs are made up of a different fiber. They are people that have shaped their personality as leaders via the repetition of good habits. Without a doubt they have the capacity to confront adverse situations and usually come out stronger than before. Some people may call this being resilient. I really do not think they know what the word "stress" means.

Two life-changing events took place in 1995. Leo was voted out as President of TelePizza, the company he had started and of which he was the single largest shareholder, without any prior notice at a shareholders meeting. Then, that same year, while I was pregnant with our third son, we received the devastating news that our second son, Andrés, needed a lifesaving liver transplant. He was born with a metabolic deficiency that caused cirrhosis of the liver. The months that we waited for a liver donor were filled with anguish, but Leo showed that he does not get overwhelmed. Instead, these problems seemed like an incentive for him to find solutions and he remained calm at all times. He always says we must concentrate on the important issues while simultaneously continuing in the right direction. Following his guidelines, our life got back on track. Our third son, Alfonso, was born in February 1996. He was a special baby, who filled us with joy. In June, Leo returned to the presidency of TelePizza. In August, Andrés received a liver transplant, at just 20 months old, thanks to the generosity of parents who had just lost their own child and a talented group of doctors at the 12 de Octubre Children's Hospital in Madrid.

Leo patiently stood by my side while I took care of our children, providing the comfort and security needed during those delicate moments. He demonstrated that he is capable of working under pressure, even though he had a number of fronts opened. Over the years, no matter how many problems he has had to confront in the business world, he never came home in a bad mood. Even though he has a strong character, he is very kind. It is common for leaders like him to have a high level of emotional intelligence. This term was made famous by Daniel Goldman, when he referred to the managerial capacity to handle one's own emotions in a healthy manner. This means not only understanding your own emotions but others' as well. It is important that problems not cloud one's view so that leaders can make the right decision every time.

During that time period, after being forced out of the presidency, many of the people we thought of as family and some as friends turned out to be traitors. Their behavior did not alter Leo's composure. On the other hand, we were filled with satisfaction from the support provided by a group of five TelePizza employees who stood by our side during those nine months, even though they were putting their jobs on the line. Loyalty and friendship are qualities that Leo appreciates, is thankful for and reciprocates.

My composure was less serene because I suffered as a witness to the injustice committed against my husband, the founder of TelePizza, by all the other shareholders, a number of top executives, and one of Leo's own family members. In addition, I was affected by the pain and sorrow caused by seeing our son Andrés sick and my inability to be present with our other two children, since we spent an enormous amount of time at the hospital. Since that time, Leo and I have worked with and funded teams of medical researchers in the hope that they can find a cure for this deficiency.

Another important characteristic that I consider crucial in leaders is the absence of fear, or the ability to conquer it via quick actions and transmitting self-confidence to those around them. It is a quality that on occasions can make them look like daredevils or risk takers. Fear is just an excuse. Fear, excuses, and complaints are not part of Leo's vocabulary. Additionally, I believe that leaders possess a substantial amount of intuitive intelligence, because they are capable of making decisions and properly defining what is really important in a short amount of time. They see what others do not see, they implement strategies that others consider impossible to implement, and they are open to new ways of doing things. They are constantly thinking outside the box. For them there is no such thing as the outside of a comfort zone, because being outside the comfort zone is so normal for them. If we add that these individuals possess a high intelligence quotient (I found out Leo's level of intelligence when I gave him the tests), and we add to this great persistence and an unlimited capacity for work, they have all the necessary ingredients to be successful in every project, more often than not.

Up until now, through a brief description of how Leo and I met and our first years of marriage, I have tried to define, in my opinion, how an entrepreneur behaves. Most likely there are parents that during the reading of this book will recognize some of these leadership qualities in their own children. These young men and women are needed in society, and they will most likely need the understanding and support of their friends and family members in order to achieve their dreams. Leo firmly believes, and I have mentioned it previously, that an entrepreneur is not born but is self-made through learning the appropriate skills and developing good habits. He believes success in life is fulfilling one's dreams. He himself is a walking example of this. Those people with the entrepreneurial mentality who are about to embark on a new venture, opening a business or starting a project, will find in this book suggestions, advice and ideas that will help them be successful. In these pages, they will read what is not taught in many universities, because "Shoot for the Stars and You Will Land on the Moon" is the result of his own experience, which Leo calls the university of life or the school of hard knocks. It is the sum of the hands-on knowledge acquired in each stage of his career. I simply call it wisdom.

As the wife of an entrepreneur, I can tell you that it has been essential for me to be flexible. In fact, if I had to choose one word to describe my life next to an entrepreneur, it would be *change*. My routine is one of constant and continuous change. Adaptability has been my model, as it would have been impossible for me to follow Leo without it. Entrepreneurs like Leo vary their ways and alter strategies as many times as needed in order to fulfill their vision. Once they achieve it, they are already thinking of their next project. The dream is the motor that sparks a passion, almost obsessively, to put in practice an idea that many times are forged in their dreams while sleeping. They have trained their minds to respond at any moment, including in their sleep, to the question: *how?* It has also been essential for me to encourage Leo's enthusiasm, or at least, not to discourage it. Entrepreneurs do not leave their uniforms at work, but on the contrary, when they arrive at home they continue being the same intense, perfectionist person. In our house, he remains the same tireless, passionate, creative, demanding person that he is at work.

I am convinced that the visionary entrepreneur cannot be stopped, but I also believe that they need the support of their loved ones. They relax briefly after finishing one project and starting a new one, since their minds are constantly active. In the case of Leo I have been able to observe that he is capable of managing a number of projects at the same time, and I have always been surprised by his memory and his capacity to relate facts and concepts simultaneously.

When he asked me to write the prologue to his book, whose title I believe he has chosen well, I felt that, as always, he was including me in this new dream. As a wife, this is something that I have always appreciated.

Those who know him personally will never forget his intense personality, which is sometimes overpowering, charismatic, but never two-faced. He is authentic and behaves in the same manner no matter whom he is addressing. Even those who do not know him in person have probably witnessed the creation and evolution of TelePizza. Many of today's adults grew up eating those tasty pizzas during their adolescent years. There will be others that will remember Leo as the Chairman of Jazztel. It was a struggling company in which he invested financial resources and energy, first to make it viable and then successful.

There have been many problems, tense moments, and at times little reason for hope. The criticism he received could have demoralized many, but he continued with the mission of rescuing Jazztel by hiring outstanding directors and the right chief executive officer. Displaying his sense of humor, he calls those executives the *cableros*, which is a Spanish term of endearment for cable experts. In reality, I have never seen my husband give up, no matter how difficult things became. As a curious anecdote, I can add that he has never used a computer, even though he and his iPad have become inseparable. We, my children and I, have shown him how to use it. Nevertheless, he says all businesses are guided by the same principles, independent of the product or service that they provide. I have been witness to many hours of hard work, dedication, patience, intuition, creativity, investments, and many difficult decisions in a very risky marketplace. These are the principles he used to grow TelePizza and Jazztel into members of the prestigious IBEX 35 index, representing the most liquid companies on the Madrid Stock Exchange.

When I asked Leo why he wanted to write this book, he mentioned two main reasons. The first is his desire to leave a legacy for his descendants. This book is not only full of Leo's life experiences, but also the process he followed for his personal self-development and how he became the man he is today. The second reason is to motivate and encourage young people. He advocates that it is possible to make your dreams come true in this world, this democratic world, where there are equal opportunities for all. I have heard him advise many people that we should never give up nor accept being complacent. Leo was born having everything, grew up enjoying it all and matured in his teens when his family lost everything. However, he chose a path of courage, hard work and persistence, instead of a path of self-pity, in order to build back what Fidel Castro's regime stole from his parents.

Last but not least, I wish to say that next to him I have learned to enjoy being part of his dreams. Today, I love a country that is not mine, Cuba, because he has transmitted to me his wish to see a Cuba Libre, a free Cuba. I have never visited the island, but it has been sufficient to have had the honor to know many brave men and women with exemplary principles. Their spouses have the same courage and lived without having them at their side, so that they could dedicate their lives to liberating their homeland from a totalitarian dictatorship.

We are proud of the five children, all of them men, intelligent, capable, honest yet humble. Even though they have two different mothers and an age difference between them, they have a wonderful relationship based on their love and respect for each other. The five deserve much credit, because they all have a very successful father that raises the bar, the benchmark, and they must each strive to shine on their own. The two older sons are successful professionals in their respective careers, they have chosen their wives wisely, and they are the parents of our wonderful grandchildren. Our three younger sons are finishing their educations and starting out their careers. They are talented, creative and ambitious. My husband and I are both convinced that they will all succeed in their chosen fields. I do not know of an entrepreneur who has found happiness if they have failed in their family life. All those dreams achieved during their lifetime gain meaning, if they manage to stand the test of time and are passed on from generation to generation.

1

LEAVING CUBA

The second Sunday of July 1960 started like any other, but the events of that day dramatically changed my entire life.

I was 13 years old, living a youthful and innocent life in Cuba, completely unaware of the term *communism* and especially of the impact it would have on my country and my whole family.

I remember all the details as if it were yesterday. My friend Agustin Arellano's family was driving me to my family's home in Miramar, a suburb of Havana, after a visit to his parents' rice plantation. It was a long car ride, with little traffic from the Pinar del Rio province near the town of Artemisa. We had the windows down, enjoying the warm, tropical breeze which carried the aroma of the season's sugar cane harvest.

As the car pulled into the driveway and I entered our home, my parents frantically whisked me into my father's library. It was a room that I had only been in once before. It was totally off limits to me and my brothers, because it was my father's place for solitude, leisure and reading. In this formal setting, I knew it could only be bad news.

The words that followed were abrupt and direct. My father, who was a well regarded lawyer in Havana stated, "Your uncle Raúl has gone into exile and flew to the United States this morning. The family had heard rumors that Fidel Castro's new regime was planning to arrest him."

I was speechless, and before I could say anything my mother spoke, "We are worried," she said. "The violence is not over. You and your two brothers will be flying to Florida where we know you will be safe. Your uncle and his family will meet you there."

My father informed me that two of us would fly to Miami on July 13, and the other one on July 18 accompanying my grandmother Romelia. She was to stay the extra days to attend my cousin Graciela Pujals' wedding on July 16 in Havana.

I loved my grandmother and quickly volunteered to fly with her on the later flight. Twenty months a widow, she and my grandfather had been married 48 years before he passed away on November 8, 1958, less than two months before Fidel Castro rose to power. Even in those moments of immense surprise it seemed incredible to me that two people who had spent almost every day together for five decades would now have two completely different fates. My grandfather would never know what happened to Cuba. My grandmother was now leaving the country and would live the bitter experience of being in exile until she passed away, 24 years later.

My parents did not believe that a communist regime was possible in Cuba. Hardly anyone did. We were ninety miles away from the most vibrant democracy and powerful capitalist economy in the world. Our standard of living was as high as any European country and the people longed for peace and prosperity.

In hindsight, as Castro marched seven days from the eastern provinces to Havana on January 7, 1959, there was at least one person who saw the writing on the wall. Years later, my dad told me the story of a Hungarian man who was renting an apartment from my family. On January 10, just three days after Fidel Castro triumphantly entered Havana, the Hungarian tenant gave notice to my parents that he was leaving the country at the end of the month and would be canceling his rental agreement. He clearly stated his reason for wanting to leave so suddenly: "In Hungary I suffered through a communist totalitarian dictatorship and I do not want to repeat the experience."

He further explained the similarities to what he had seen in Hungary that gave him the chills. There were revolutionaries with long hair and beards. They had catholic rosaries hung around their necks, projecting an image of kindness and holiness. Yet, they marched with weapons as a show of strength and, as the revolutionaries had in Hungary, were continually waving red and black flags.

Of course, the Hungarian was right. His instinct had been sharpened by his own personal experience.

Over the years, I have noticed that normal democratic citizens who wish to live in harmony, like my parents, do not comprehend that some politicians are eager to gain power by promoting class warfare pitting the poor against the rich.

Even in the wake of a revolution that had seen the dictator Fulgencio Batista flee Cuba, decent Cubans were unprepared for the class warfare that was coming.

In this context, three months after Batista and the Hungarian had left the country, Cuba still was not safe. Castro promised democratic elections, freedom, and progress. These were lies and empty promises. Many rebels who had risen up against Batista in support of Castro turned against him. In the months following March 1959, they set up guerilla camps in the Escambray mountain range in the center of the island, while violence flared in the City of Havana. It was not uncommon to hear about bombs exploding in movie theaters or other acts of sabotage against the regime.

My parents became convinced that a new revolution was going to take place against Fidel Castro's new government. Now, they could see the writing on the wall and they were concerned for our safety.

The new government was moving at high speed toward a totalitarian dictatorship. They enacted laws like the Agrarian Reform decree to control labor independence. They nationalized large companies, and created a Soviet-style State Agency called the Central Planning Board (JUCEPLAN).

Many guerilla leaders began denouncing Castro as a populist and a liar who was maneuvering on a daily basis to set up a dictatorship with the support of the so-called socialist camp. This opposition gave the Cuban people hope for democracy, but suddenly these key rebel leaders began disappearing. For example, beloved Commander Camilo Cienfuegos supposedly died in a plane crash. The remains of the plane were never found. Other leaders were subjected to summary trials and sentenced to long-term imprisonment.

This happened to Huber Matos, a commander of the revolution, who was sentenced to 20 years in prison, and Mario Chanes de Armas, who was sentenced to 30 years. Ironically, years earlier, on July 26, 1953, Chanes de Armas had stood next to Castro in one of the first uprisings against Batista, the attack on the Moncada barracks. They each served nearly two years in the Isle of Pines prison, but received pardons. Following their release, Fidel, Mario and others traveled to Mexico to raise funds, organize, and plan the guerilla warfare strategies to be implemented a year later in the revolution. They, numbering 82 guerilla fighters, traveled on the yacht *Granma*, landing on the southeastern part of the island of Cuba, and headed into the Sierra Maestra mountain range in December 1956 to launch an offensive against Batista's army.

We had one family member who became involved in the new Castro government. My great-aunt Elena Mederos Cabañas was a direct descendant of

Cuban-born collaborators with Jose Marti in the Cuban War of Independence (1895-1898). She was a charitable woman who had dedicated her life to helping the poor and needy in Cuba. In recognition of her good deeds she was named to the newly formed cabinet as Secretary of Social Welfare in January 1959. She resigned six months later over objections to Castro's policies, such as the thousands of assassinations being carried out by firing squads after summary trials. Subsequently she became active in clandestine movements against the new dictatorship. She went into exile in 1961 and continued advocating for freedom in Cuba through a Washington-based nonprofit organization, Of Human Rights, until she passed away in 1981.

My brothers and I maintained complete silence about our impending departure from the island at our parents' request. Leaving Cuba was not as simple as buying a ticket and getting on a plane. The authorities controlled departures and keeping quiet was essential to avoiding problems at the airport.

In the meantime, life continued as usual. We continued our usual social outings, and as difficult as it was, I did not tell any of my friends at the Havana Yacht Club about our plans. I left without saying goodbye to anyone. Years later I learned that I was not the only one of my schoolmates keeping this big secret. Schools the following year saw more and more desks abruptly abandoned each week.

At our home, we told the staff that we would return in a month, at the end of August. That return has yet to occur. I appreciated them very much and thought of them often, wondering if they adapted to the poverty that is widespread in every communist country. In exile, only one of our employees, Felicia "Titi" Guerra, our Jamaican cook who had known me since I was born, sent yearly letters to my father. I was very fond of Titi. I often snuck into the kitchen to be with her as she taught me to prepare my favorite dishes, especially my weekend breakfast.

She asked my father for financial assistance, which he provided. After my father died, I took over sending her money, until she passed away. Now I help her daughter, whom I have only known through letters and videos that she has sent me. I hope to meet her one day.

On July 13, my brothers flew to Miami, along with my aunt Alicia and several cousins. My grandmother and I waited until after Graciela's wedding, which took place at Corpus Christi Catholic Church in Havana. The reception was held in the backyard of our family compound, which comprised of four houses built by my maternal grandfather, Francisco Pujals Claret. It was a celebration that was typical of our times in pre-communist Cuba, surrounded by family, friends, love, and laughter. I remember keeping my cousin's German shepherd, named Silver, away from the guests at our home. The fondness I had for Silver has carried on, and I still breed German shepherd dogs of the work line in Spain.

On the days leading up to my flight, the repression was showing its ugly side and the violence was raging. Daily shootings took place in La Cabaña fortress and other military barracks. A climate of terror swept the country that continues to this day. Cubans, newly arrived in the United States after having suffered many years under the dictatorship, say with, almost the same words, that Castro has put the fear of living in a police state "in the mind" of every citizen. Fear is so engrained in their minds that they prefer risking their lives on makeshift rafts through shark-infested waters rather than staying in Cuba and facing the regime. The highly publicized case of Elian Gonzalez and his family is just one of thousands of such cases.

On July 18, I arrived with my mother, father, and grandmother at the airport. I knew there were three gold watches hidden in my luggage. They were the only things of sentimental and monetary value that I was able to stow. Saying goodbye to my parents on that day in the "fishbowl" of Rancho Boyeros Airport is an experience that I will never forget. Through the window I saw my mother, who had a strange look of sorrow on her face. It was a look I could never describe with words.

2

My Exile in Florida

My first week in Miami felt like a vacation. We stayed at my aunt Olga's house, which overlooked picturesque, serene Biscayne Bay. We spent those first days fishing, laughing and playing, as kids do.

The honeymoon period in Miami was short lived and the reality that I was living in exile soon set in. It felt as if we had just taken a huge step backwards and my impression was that my life in Miami was light-years behind what I had left in Havana.

What a difference a communist revolution makes! It is astonishing and sad that today Miami is a world-class city and a symbol of Cuban achievement, while Havana is impoverished and in ruins.

We left my aunt's beautiful home and moved into a rented house in a lower-middle-class neighborhood in the northwest section of Fort Lauderdale. We were five boys living in close quarters, all brothers and cousins, all of us grandchildren of the Pujals-Mederos marriage, my mother's parents.

We lived with Uncle Raúl and Aunt Alice, my maternal grandmother's youngest daughter. I slept on a plastic cot every night. I remember lying there, devastated by the abrupt turn my life had just taken. Every night for the first month, I cried myself to sleep, quietly, so that no one could hear me. Looking back, I know those tears were part of accepting my new life. The pain strengthened and hardened me.

The next time I cried was 11 years later, when my mother passed away of a cardiac arrest, on August 25, 1971. I was in the U.S. Army, serving in the Vietnam War.

I have vivid memories of a few events that happened during those early years in the United States. One of them was Hurricane Donna (in Cuba we called them cyclones), in late August of 1960. It was the first time I had experienced such a huge natural disaster. Winds exceeded 140 mph and sounded like a freight train driving through the middle of a rock concert. Rain came through all the window cracks, soaking our tiny home. We had only been in Fort Lauderdale one month. What a warm, and very wet, welcome!

The main industry in the city was tourism. During the winter, South Florida was the preferred destination of Americans from the Northeast. Curiously, at Easter, the beaches were full of university students. The Easter break lasted an entire month, because universities observed the holiday during different weeks. It was a unique social event and very appealing. A city with a population of approximately 50,000 people became, during those 30 days, home to half a million people, sleeping and staying wherever they could. The presence of these young students, with their special manner of enjoyment, became the basis for the 1961 film *Where the Boys Are*.

In September 1960, my brothers and I enrolled at Central Catholic High School, which was headed by Dominican nuns. It was the only Catholic school in that city. My younger brother and cousins attended Saint Clements Elementary School. It quickly dawned on me that I was not in Havana anymore. School was conducted in English, which I did not yet speak fluently!

To make matters worse, there was a significant difference in social standing. In Havana, my last names were recognized and respected. In Fort Lauderdale, I felt that I was just a number, another exile now living in the United States.

I remember my mother saying, "They stole all our possessions, but they cannot steal what we have in our heads. We have to use what we have."

I took school seriously. I had already completed my first year of high school in Cuba, but I was only 13 years old so they recommended that I repeat my freshman year. I excelled in algebra. I remember always calling out the answer before the teacher could even finish writing the equation. This resulted in quite a few glaring looks and reprimands from the teacher.

In English class, I stayed quiet, and when the teacher asked me a question, I would respond with, "No speak English." After a while, she saw straight through this and knew that I understood more than I let on. One day, the nun rebuked me, saying, "You do understand and speak English!" It was because of her that I had to give up my comfortable silence during English class. What a nun!

Almost as dramatically different as the language was the fact that Central Catholic was a co-ed high school. I was not used to having girls sitting alongside me in class in Cuba, as I had always attended all-boys schools belonging to the Order of the La Salle brothers.

It did not take long for puppy love to take hold, as I set my eyes on my first American girlfriend, a cute blonde girl. We went to the movies together, and I even had my first kiss with her. Suddenly, I began to think that maybe America was not so bad after all.

Unlike in Miami, few Cuban families lived in Fort Lauderdale. Despite this fact, I somehow ran into two of my former classmates from the La Salle School in Cuba, Florentino and Eduardo Blanco. I had not seen them since leaving the island. It was so refreshing to be with friends who understood me because they had experienced the same uprooting I had. Unfortunately, the following year they moved to Costa Rica, where their parents had decided to start a new life.

We took comfort in a few new hobbies, like collecting Top Value Stamps, which were given to supermarket customers. When you collected a certain number of stamps, you could redeem them for merchandise. The first thing we got was a set of electric shears for cutting hair. With six men living in the same house, we realized that this purchase would save us $9 per month. While this might not sound like much today, one must keep in mind, at that time the minimum wage was just one dollar per hour.

My uncle Raúl decided to play the role of barber, and my brother Eduardo was the first guinea pig. Suffice it to say it did not go well. When my uncle was finished, the outline on the back of my brother's head looked like a map of Africa. I convinced my brother to let me try to fix the mess. I had such success that I became the official house barber! It was my first profession, although initially I did not receive any compensation. My reputation was such that some of our relatives in Miami even drove to our home, so that I could cut their hair. I was proud of my work and pleased that I was saving them money. As time passed, they started paying me $1.00 for every haircut. Everyone was happy.

At the end of 1960, when the small amount of money that my parents were able to get out of Cuba was nearly used up, my mother decided to leave the island and find work in Florida. She was quickly hired at an architectural firm. She had been the first woman to graduate from the architectural school of the University of Pennsylvania, in 1940. When she returned to Cuba, her degree was accredited by

Havana University, and in 1941 and she became the first female professor at the School of Architecture. When she left Cuba, she had the position of assistant dean of the architecture school.

Haircuts aside, I found it very difficult to live in a small house with so many people. My father foresaw that this would happen. He had said, "In a house, you can accommodate a lot of furniture, curtains, paintings, and rugs, but not too many characters with different personalities."

I know that my father was mostly referring to me and my personality. I found it especially hard to accept my uncle Raúl's often illogical reprimands. I remember one confrontation very vividly. My uncle forced my younger brother to eat tomato slices. He obeyed but then threw up what he had swallowed. Then my uncle tried to force my brother to eat what he had just vomited, and I decided to confront him, saying something along the lines of "Over my dead body!" For this outburst in defense of my brother, I was punished.

In the fall of 1960, our small rented house seemed inadequate, so my aunt and uncle decided to buy a house. The following year, my mother, who was sleeping in my grandmother Romelia's room, decided that it was time for us to buy our own home. Wanting to keep the family together, she bought a house a hundred yards away from my aunt and uncle's house. Our new home was located at 2331 SW 31st Avenue, in Fort Lauderdale.

I got my driver's license at the age of 14 but could only drive if an adult accompanied me. I wanted to earn money, so I got a job delivering newspapers at 5 AM. My intention was to use my bicycle to deliver the newspapers, but my mother did not allow me to leave the house alone at that early hour, so she offered to accompany me in her car. On the second day delivering newspapers, I got into an accident. My mother had exited the car and left the door open. I put the car in reverse with the door open and crashed the car door into a mailbox.

She convinced me to look for another activity, so I dedicated myself to doing odd jobs around the neighborhood, cutting grass and repairing things for the neighbors. My mother always had more than one job. She worked as a teacher at St. Thomas Aquinas, which was formerly Central Catholic High School. She taught Spanish and mechanical drawing. In the evenings, she designed houses for a construction company that was busy taking advantage of the booming home construction market serving the growing population of South Florida.

There was progress in our new lives in the United States. Nevertheless, my father continued to live in Cuba and traveled back and forth to visit us in Fort Lauderdale almost monthly. He naively thought that if he maintained a presence in Cuba, the regime would not confiscate our home. Unfortunately, he was wrong.

On August 4, 1961, he decided to stay in Fort Lauderdale for good. The regime had issued a new currency and no matter how much of the old currency you had, it was exchangeable for just 200 of the new pesos. This meant that all of the money that people might have saved, deposited in the bank or even had hidden away had no value whatsoever. Overnight, the government made everyone poor with the stoke of a pen.

I remember that before leaving Cuba in 1960 my parents bought plane tickets for us to fly to many countries around the world. The real purpose of this was to convert the tickets into dollars when we left the country in order to recuperate the cash. Once they were in exile, they learned that that those tickets bought in Cuba could not be returned or exchanged for cash.

Around that same time, the repressive forces of the regime captured my uncle José, my mother's brother, and his whereabouts were unknown. I remember that my father went to the CIA office in Miami to volunteer to return to Cuba and find out the whereabouts of my uncle. However, the official with whom he met told him, "If you return to Cuba, there will be two prisoners instead of one."

In Cuba, my father was a respected lawyer and notary who owned his own firm. In America he could not practice his profession, because the law in Cuba is based on the Napoleonic code, and in the United States the law is based on the U.S. Constitution, legislation and English common law.

He accepted a low-paying job as a delivery driver for a dental laboratory. After the missile crisis in October 1962, he realized that our exile was going to be a long one. He sent his résumé out to various private schools in New England with the hopes of becoming a Spanish teacher. He was offered a position on the faculty of Suffield Academy, in Suffield, Connecticut.

In September 1963, as I was about to start the new school year, I went on a journey with my father that I will never forget, riding a bus for 30 hours, from Fort Lauderdale, Florida, to Hartford, Connecticut. It was an uncomfortable trip, to say the least, and seemingly never-ending. Even as a teenager, the journey caused swollen ankles.

My father's compensation package included my tuition, so I would finish high school at the very prestigious Suffield Academy.

***

Obviously, living in exile was a difficult time in my life, which is why I always find it fascinating that some people romanticize Cuba. In my opinion, a good gauge of the quality of a country's government is the number of people who emigrate versus the number of those who immigrate. In order to eliminate disputes about the well-being of a Cuban citizen, I always suggest that one must analyze how many people go to the island and decide to stay versus how many are disillusioned and leave. On the one hand, about 20 percent of Cuba's 11 million people have left the island. On the other I have not heard of anywhere near 2 million people moving to Cuba's communist "worker's paradise". In fact, about the only people emigrating to Cuba these days are running away from Medicare Fraud charges or even more serious crimes! It is therefore easy to gauge how real people see the present and future living on this island.

The number of Cuban exiles who have left the island and never returned nearly equals the entire population of some Central American countries. I have traveled plenty and lived in many places, but the views that some Spaniards have about Cuba has always surprised me. There are those, for example, who have the idea that living in Cuba is a continuous festival of songs and dances. These people do not realize that Cubans sing because they cannot speak freely, and if they speak against the regime, they will be imprisoned. In my opinion, these misconceptions are the result of the fever of liberal ideologies and the Castro propaganda machine.

Playa Girón, or the Bay of Pigs, began on the night of April 16, 1961, and was the first betrayal of Cuba by President John F. Kennedy. About 2,500 Cuban freedom fighters trained by the United States and promised U.S. military air support, launched an invasion of the southern part of Matanzas, a central province near Havana. Their mission was to overthrow the Castro regime, but without warning President Kennedy canceled the programmed air support that would have helped the infantry battalions. The result of that measure caused a loss of freedom for Cubans and a strengthening of the Castro regime. President Kennedy sent these men to their deaths under false pretenses, and without the slightest chance of success.

President Kennedy betrayed the Cubans a second time in late October 1962, when he signed an agreement with Nikita Khrushchev, the General Secretary of the communist party of the Soviet Union. The pact prevented Cubans from using U.S. territory to attack the Castro regime. Many exiled patriots have spent years in American prisons because they took actions to free the people of Cuba from oppression.

Today, the strategy in vogue for obtaining freedom in Cuba is via peaceful means, but I think it will be very difficult to achieve emancipation from communism with balloons and banners when the enemy is armed and shoots to kill. We have been part of an exchange in a game of chess in which players have looked for their own economic and political gains, without any noticeable interest in the freedom of all the Cuban people.

In my opinion, President Kennedy's betrayal is one of the main reasons why the majority of Cuban Americans have traditionally voted for Republican candidates. Knowing the history of democratic administrations with respect to Cuba, it is impossible for me to understand how, with few exceptions, a Cuban patriot anxious to see his country free could vote for a politician of the Democratic Party.

3

SOME MEMORIES OF CUBA

Like any child away from his home, I was homesick for my country. People often say that it is easier for children to adapt to new situations than adults. This may be true, but my early years in the United States were difficult and often sad for me.

By comparison, I have only good memories of my childhood in Cuba. For most Cubans, March 10, 1952, when Fulgencio Batista staged a coup, Cuba's future changed. I did not immediately experience any interruption in my daily life, except for the heated political discussions between my father and mother at dinner. The subject was always the same: my parents were worried about the dictatorship and felt Cuba needed to return to a genuine rule of law.

While there were countless things I missed about Cuba, I especially missed my family's farmland, as I have always had, even to this day, a passion for farming and livestock. Whenever I visited a farm in Cuba, I felt like I was breathing pure air. I dreamed that one day I would have a farm of my own. I loved the country side and felt free and alive playing in open spaces.

I still remember what should have been a great childhood accomplishment: the first time that I rode a bicycle without the training wheels! I was pedaling at a furious speed, trying to catch my friend Eddy Sardiñas. Suddenly, he slowed down to go around a corner. I had not yet mastered stepping on the brakes and crashed into the back of his bicycle. I flew through the air and my two front teeth were knocked out as I landed head first on the pavement. I bled a lot, and I had to wait patiently for my permanent teeth to grow in. Eddie survived the incident without a scrape, and incidentally, would later become a noteworthy executive himself as President of the Bacardi Company in the United States.

Many of my family members owned farms, including my grandmother Romelia and my great-aunt Elena Mederos. My mother, recognizing my interest in agriculture, once told me that she had insisted to her mother that I should be considered to inherit one of her farms. This would have helped me fulfill my dream of becoming an agricultural engineer, my career of choice had the family not gone into exile.

In Havana, I loved helping our gardener, Julian, cut the grass, water the plants, and remove weeds from the grass beds. In the corner of the garden, I even planted several crops of tomatoes, beans, and corn. I loved to nurture them and watch them grow each day.

The Sonora, a farm belonging to my aunt Elena Mederos, was located near Havana, so we would go there on weekends frequently. She and her husband, Hilario González, got along very well with my parents. Hilario and Elena were joyful and communicative, and they enjoyed being with our family. The farm had many mango trees and mangos are one of my favorite fruits.

I first learned to ride horses on a farm named Niña Sierra, which was located along the boundary that separates the provinces of Havana and Matanzas. It was about 600 acres and was owned by my grandmother Romelia.

At The Sonora, we would also ride horses and one afternoon I had a serious accident, falling off and losing consciousness. This did not stop me from riding again. I never stopped enjoying riding horses. In fact, for the last twenty years I have been breeding horses and it is one of my great passions.

My uncle José began his career as an entrepreneur with a herd of 100 dairy cows at the Niña Sierra farm. When visiting that farm, I learned from the farmhands how to milk cows. I was a free spirited child and also enjoyed searching for hen's nests, where they would lay their eggs. My uncle's dairy trucks, under the brand of Santa Ana, distributed our fresh milk in glass bottles, which were chilled between large pieces of dry ice during delivery. They were not pasteurized, so before drinking the milk, each household would have to boil it three times in order to kill the bacteria.

My grandmother's largest farm was called Jejenes and had an area of 10,660 acres and about 5,000 head of zebu cattle, the kind famous for the large humps on their backs. It was located in the province of Pinar del Río. Every summer, I would spend about 10 days there. On the Jejenes farm I learned to lasso small calves, the same way that it is done in U.S. rodeos. I was pretending to be a real cowboy!

I wondered how I would turn this passion into a moneymaking career. Later, in exile, I asked my uncle Francis, my mother's elder brother, how he earned his money on the farm. He explained that every year about 1,200 calves were born, which at 1 year of age would weigh about 500 pounds. The per-pound price of the yearling was about 20 cents, or about $100 per cow. It was clear to me that I would not become a millionaire as a cattle breeder in Cuba, but my motivation was not to get rich. I simply loved the idea of breeding cattle!

In Cuba, we lived in a family compound of sorts, with all of our houses close together on the same property. In the backyard of one of the houses my uncle Raúl, a civil engineer, built a dollhouse. His daughters, Alicia and María Elena, who were a year and a year and a half younger than me, played with their dolls there for hours and hours. I remember, one afternoon, my uncle came home from work and saw me playing in the dollhouse with his daughters and asked me, "Why are you in here?"

I responded, "In every house there must be a man in charge of the household." My uncle nodded and allowed us to continue playing.

Another interesting moment that I recall was the day my younger brother was born. My parents, thinking he was going to be a girl, had chosen the name Elena. When they found out it was a boy, my mother asked my brother and I to decide on a new name. I was about 3 years old and our decision was unanimous. We would name him Eduardo, after our dear friend Eduardo Sardiñas, with whom we used to play in the park every day. Since Eduardo was born on June 13, which is the saint's day of San Antonio, he was baptized with the name of Eduardo Antonio.

Most of my childhood memories revolve around La Salle School in Miramar. I remember my first day at La Salle's Miramar kindergarten. I was 4 years old, and started early, because my older brother was no longer at home to play with me. I insisted that my mother allow me go to school with him. I was convinced that I would have fun and, indeed, that is exactly what happened.

I recall being a logical and rational student possessing common sense and a good memory. I learned enough in class that I did not have to do homework until I began high school. I paid attention to the teachers, understood what they were explaining and, thanks to the good memory that God bestowed on me (and that I inherited from my parents) I passed with good grades.

I was a good kid, but I did not escape childhood without a few altercations. I remember fighting a boy named Gastón Godoy Angulo. He was the son of an important politician who later served as Minister of Justice during the dictatorship of Fulgencio Batista. Before the blows became too serious, we were separated and punished by facing the wall in separate corners of the classroom. Gastón and I ended up becoming good friends.

I remember very well how much I enjoyed school recesses. Every month a new game became fashionable, and all of the students played it, whatever it was. At one point in time it was marbles. I had dozens of crystal balls and several made of stainless steel. The object of marbles is to win, the reward for which is winning more marbles. I was pretty good at the game and often won, so my collection of marbles continually grew.

Then, suddenly, we began to play spinning tops, watching them dance or trying to split the other student's top. Then came the Hula-Hoop, and everybody worldwide used their hips to keep those plastic rings at the waist. Stilts were also very popular, and we used to race with them. Yo-yos had their moment, too, and they always had to be one of the Duncan brand models.

We used to play baseball and a game that we called "Burn You" with a European soccer ball. All of these games became a part of our lives during recess at our elementary school.

Every year, the school organized bicycle races. This was a big deal. Each school grade had various heats, and the winners participated in the final race for each grade. The preliminary heat was about 600 yards around the large perimeter of the school backyard, and then the finals were two laps around the same field. I was now a skilled cyclist and one year I won my heat and moved on to the finals with 10 others who had won their preliminary heats. My bicycle was a hand me down from my older brother and I needed a faster bike for the final. A friend loaned his bicycle to me and I made good use of it. During the first lap I stayed behind the first place racer until there were only 200 yards left. I had saved my energy and I gave it all the strength that I had left. At the last moment I passed him, and I won the race by perhaps 10 yards.

At the end of the school year, they gave the bicycle race awards, and the brothers of La Salle School chose Gustavo Machado, also known as Cawy, as the winner. He was one of the sons of the owners of the soft drink factory of the same name. I complained to my mother that I had won the race, and she replied, "Talk to the brother responsible for your classroom."

So I did. To my surprise, he answered that I led the race only for the final stretch, whereas my opponent had been ahead for the first 1,000 yards of the race. I am sure that you are as surprised reading this as I was hearing it!

I had something taken from me that I had earned, and through this I learned that life is not as fair as I had thought.

This is not a reason to be unfair yourself. Only to exercise caution when dealing with others, who are more often than not motivated by self-interest. I have always tried to be fair with everybody, especially with all of the employees who have worked with me and depended upon fairness in our dealings.

Another thing I remember are the street vendors that came to our schools. They sold Spanish fritters called *churros*, fried and sprinkled with sugar. They also served hot, tasty warm croquettes and guava pastries. Those street vendors made our day when we came out hungry for recess. We probably made their day, too, because every student bought something!

At noon, I enjoyed going home for lunch on the school bus. Our housemaids loved us three brothers very much, and I remember that they liked to sing. We lived in a very healthy, cheerful atmosphere. At noontime, I used to listen to the adventures of "Los Tres Villalobos" (Rodolfo, Miguelón, and Machito) on the radio, which was a very entertaining program for children. I tried not to miss an episode. After the afternoon school session, I normally played with my brothers and cousins until dinner time.

When I was in exile, my old friend Agustín Arellano reminded me of some stories from our time at Colegio de La Salle in the Vedado neighborhood. We were between 11 and 12 years old. Sometimes we snuck out of school a little early in order to be the first ones to reach Línea Street. There we asked for a botella. Basically, we hitchhiked to our houses to have lunch. We lived very close to each other and after lunch we loved to play basketball, or whatever was in fashion at the time together. We had more autonomy than most of our classmates, who went to school by bus or private car, and that made us feel older.

Agustín also reminded me of a decree of the La Salle school director, "LaSallistas, you must shine above the anonymous majority." On numerous occasions that phrase has come to mind. We were raised to shine.

Another friend at the time, Alfonso Cueto, known as Proton to his friends, reminded me years later that even as a child I was always more focused than the rest of my friends and colleagues. For example, when we finished the basketball workouts, I did not go with them to the beach, but stayed on, practicing.

I remember swimming at Havana Yacht Club competitions. It was my aunt Mercedes who convinced me to sign up. Her daughter Graciela swam with the team of the Havana Biltmore Yacht and Country Club, and began to excel in various events. In 1958 and 1959 she was elected athlete of the year and was going to go to the Rome Olympics of 1960. She decided to stop participating in competitions in order to marry Rubén Rodríguez Walling, who later, in exile, became Chairman and Chief Executive Officer of the Bacardi Company.

At the Havana Yacht Club I got to compete in the breaststroke, and I did fairly well. But it was not all roses. I also remember how hard it was to learn how to dive headfirst into the swimming pool. I decided to kneel at the edge of the pool and let gravity do the rest. Eventually I won the fight against fear. From then on, it was easier to dive into the swimming pool standing up.

I think that everyone is afraid of more than one thing, but we must overcome our own fears in order to move forward. That was a first step in finding out how to do it. Since I was very young, I learned to get out of my comfort zone and to confront the unknown. That is how I conquered fear, and I have never allowed fear to conquer me.

At the Havana Yacht Club, in addition to swimming, I practiced other sports. I took boxing and judo classes. We used to play squash and basketball and also participated in sailing and rowing classes. Competitions were organized within the club and also against other clubs in Havana known as the "Big Five," the five most important clubs in Havana.

My father would give me 10 cents for shining every pair of shoes in the house. With that money I bought comic books. My favorites were *The Exemplary Life of Catholic Saints*, the *Lone Ranger*, and *Tarzan*. I liked to collect them and regretted so much that I had to leave them in Cuba when we went into exile.

After leaving Cuba, my parents still discussed Cuban politics at the dinner table frequently. I recall one discussion in Fort Lauderdale when I really spoke up and gave my opinion. My parents were complaining that Cuba had already been through a dictatorship with Batista and now another one with Fidel Castro. I said that all those Cubans, even the ethical and patriotic, were to blame for Fidel overthrowing the government, because the professional and ethical business class did not want to get involved in politics themselves.

My parents thought politicians were corrupt and they did not want to tarnish our family names by becoming involved in the political process. I said that since honest professionals did not want to participate, the door had been left open to Batista and Castro. That is why the Cuban people suffered their misfortune.

Most parents want their children and grandchildren to enjoy more opportunities than they had. That was the case with my ancestors, who came the island of Cuba with dreams of prospering economically and hopefully starting and raising a family. They succeeded and laid the foundations for future generations to live privileged lives. I was lucky to be part of a family that had two, four, or even six generations on the island. Most of my ancestors studied at universities at a time when higher education was not the norm. They truly lived the Cuban dream, but the dream did not last long. The struggle of the Cuban people to end the Batista dictatorship brought another, even worse regime than the first.

There was no doubt in my mind that if my ancestors, thanks to their effort and dedication, had achieved economic stability and peace of mind for their descendants in the Republic of Cuba, I, more than one century later and living in exile, had to do the same, starting from scratch. I was determined to do so without complaining about the dictatorship or the wealth that we owned during our time on the island that had been confiscated. My objective was to offer my children what my parents had offered me.

4

SUFFIELD ACADEMY

Even though my father accepted a teaching position at Suffield Academy, our family home continued to be in Florida. My mother was a teacher and an architect there, so my father would be going back and forth between Fort Lauderdale and Connecticut. I went with my father to finish my last year of high school at Suffield.

We arrived on Labor Day in 1963. In the United States, Labor Day falls on the first weekend in September and is generally considered the end of summer. A little known fact is that Labor Day is a global holiday that is celebrated everywhere else in the world in the spring time on May 1, irrespective of whether it falls on a Tuesday, Thursday, or Sunday. The United States government changed this and made it a three-day weekend to honor the work and not the worker. The result is that the workers in America treat it as a holiday weekend and do not participate in marches. In this small way, the U.S. government preempted general strikes in America.

The trees in Connecticut during autumn are beautiful. The color of the leaves change from green to burgundy, burnt orange, mustard yellow, and mahogany brown, before eventually falling to the ground. As picturesque as the changing colors of the leaves are, during that time of the year most students, myself included, resent those leaves, as they must be raked!

I was one of only 206 privileged students enrolled at Suffield. My first year was my senior year, even though I was just sixteen. I took trigonometry, biology, U.S. history, English, and European geography. My schedule was full, with classes until 3 PM on Monday, Tuesday, Thursday, and Friday and until noon on Wednesday and Saturday. In addition to academics, we had to play a sport every season while in school, and trained or competed every day except Sunday. For me, fall meant American football, winter was for basketball, and baseball was in spring.

My classmates were older than me, but I adjusted well. In school my biggest challenge was that my English vocabulary was limited. We had to read many books in almost all subjects, and I struggled to complete all my assignments. At 10 PM, when they called "Lights out!" I would be up another few hours to catch up on my reading with the help of a flashlight under my blanket. I was determined to keep up.

I also struggled with trigonometry. I failed every exam I took during the fall term. I had always been good at math. I could not understand what was I doing wrong. I returned home to Fort Lauderdale for the Christmas break and discussed the situation with my older brother. He noticed that in my memorization of the trigonometry theorems I had confused the plus and minus signs. The problem was easy to fix. When I returned to school after the holidays, I took the SAT in early January and got a score of 637 in math, which was above the average. When the math professor gave me the grade he asked me if I had something against him, because he did not understand how I had gotten such a high score. I found his demeanor arrogant, and I decided not to let him in on how I had fixed my trigonometry shortcomings.

I often say that my guardian angel has always protected me, and I am convinced that he will continue to do so. Several times a year, the "townies" (Suffield teenagers from the town who were not attending the Academy) would sneak onto campus and ring our school bell to wake us as a prank. The sound of the bell was unusual. It was only used for graduations or when a school team won a sporting event.

One night this happened and we all got up from our beds, ready to fight. About 40 students from our dorm ran toward the school bell. When we caught up with the townies 200 yards downhill, I realized that only one other student, Dee Hartford, was by my side. The rest had stayed back near the dorm. We were rushing straight into a beating. Luckily, one of the townies knew Dee, so we were saved from getting beaten up.

From this I had learned that not everyone follows through on big actions. To borrow an old adage, our fellow students from the dorm "had our back: way back" up the hill.

Although my family did not have much extra money, I had a small allowance. It being small, at Suffield I found it necessary to earn a little income to subsidize a vice forbidden by my father: I enjoyed smoking cigarettes.

Necessity is a powerful motivator and I began to cut my classmates' hair in return for a pack of Marlboro cigarettes. The barbershops downtown charged a buck fifty but a pack of cigarettes could be had for twenty five cents. The "enterprise" was a win-win situation for everyone, except the town barbers. I gave three to five haircuts per week, always after dinner and before study hall.

One day I gave my classmate James Rosenberg a haircut. When the time came to pay up, James said that he would pay me later. Six weeks went by, and as his hair had grown, he asked me if I would cut it again. "Sure," I said, "come over to my room after dinner." James arrived on time and plopped into the chair. However, this time I demanded to be paid in advance either two packs of Marlboros or fifty cents. James replied that he did not have either money or cigarettes. I declined to cut his hair, and that was the last time we ever spoke. He was a very intelligent young man who achieved a perfect score of 1,600 on the SAT exams and who would go on to Harvard University. Despite this intelligence, it was clear that our upbringings and values were very different. In my mind, it was not just a pack of cigarettes at stake, but a principle. Throughout my life it has never ceased to amaze me how many people do not live up to their word. Once you make a promise, it is sacred and must be kept.

Thanks to that episode, from then on I was more cautious with new people that I met. I had been taught that everyone is innocent until proven guilty. However, through my business experience I have learned to maintain reservations regarding certain individuals, and at times I look at people as being guilty until they prove their innocence. Not everything that shines is made of gold. Even so, some business associates believe, even today, that I remain a bit naive, and that I am too trusting, giving opportunities to people who do not deserve them.

My grades were fairly average, but as the school year came to a close I was accepted at Stetson University, which is in Central Florida about a thirty-minute car ride north of Orlando. To start summer break I attended several graduation parties on Long Island in New York before starting summer break. It was great fun - drinking my first beer and taking a very cold swim in the Atlantic Ocean waters off Jones Beach. More change was in the air.

When I went from Fort Lauderdale to Stetson University after the summer was over, I left a girlfriend behind. She was 15 years old, two years younger than me. While I was studying at Suffield Academy we used to write to each other almost every day, but the relationship ended when I went on to college. Now I was much closer to the family home in Fort Lauderdale and 20 minutes west of Daytona Beach, a city on the Florida east coast, far away from snowy Connecticut.

I do not want to end this chapter without mentioning that three of my five children graduated from Suffield Academy: Carlos in 1997, Alberto in 2012, and Andres in 2013. To express my gratitude for the free tuition, room, and board that I was granted, I financed the construction of a building for the Academy and dedicated Centurion Hall in honor of my father. In addition, I was a member of the Board of Trustees for a number of years.

During my tenure as a trustee I initiated and helped implement two ideas that benefited the school substantially: a leadership program and an alumni legacy program. The first helped to attract high-profile students, and the second led to an increase in the number of applications accepted from descendants of past alumni. What I had forecast turned out to be true: the 4 percent of alumni legacy students has now, 10 years later, turned into 20 percent. If multiple generations of a family graduate from the same school every member of the family feels a sentimental attachment to the Academy, and subsequently, their donations increase significantly. I believe most people in a community share the principle that money is not for putting in your pocket, but for investing in the future of society. The more a community shares a vision for the future, the more likely they are to feel their contributions are an investment.

5

STETSON UNIVERSITY

In 1964, I enrolled at Stetson University in DeLand, Florida. DeLand is a small city near Daytona Beach, famous for the Daytona 500 stock-car race. The campus is spectacular, with sprawling, powerful oak trees and dangling Spanish moss, which are flowering plants that hang down from the tree branches. It is an unforgettable sight that sticks with you throughout the years.

My first roommate was from Kentucky. He was tall, with strawberry-blond hair and he had a thick southern accent I could not understand! I wondered if maybe he was speaking a different language. At our introduction he exclaimed, "Hail!" I looked towards the window to see if frozen raindrops were falling despite the summer heat. I was so confused, I asked him to write down what he had said. Assuredly dumbfounded, he wrote down "hell."

That is when I learned that in America there are very different pronunciations for the same word, depending on whether the speaker is from the North or the South.

Another curious moment occurred when I asked him a question, to which he replied "I reckon so." I paused, as I had never heard that word. When I asked him for an explanation, he told me to go and check Webster's dictionary. So I opened my Webster's and searched for the word, but it was not there! He confirmed that it was spelled r-e-c-k-o-n but the word was not listed in the dictionary. He was as puzzled as I was and grabbed the dictionary in amazement to see for himself. He explained to me that its meaning was along the lines of "I think so" and that in any case he would continue to use the word as it was normally accepted and used back home.

Here I was, in the United States, having spoken the English language for only four years, confronting a U.S.-born American citizen on his word usage. I reached the conclusion that this was an expression from the South, as I had not heard it used in Fort Lauderdale or in Connecticut. In addition, I became aware of the process as to how words, when used frequently by people, can ultimately become accepted by the professional ruling bodies and eventually appear, as happened in this case, in an official dictionary.

There were other cultural differences between North and South that shocked me. In 1964, there were different public bathrooms, not just for men and women but also for blacks and whites. This was something I had never seen in Cuba. It was the same for water fountains, one for whites and one for blacks. The southern states had simply not evolved in their way of thinking.

Fortunately, this policy was eliminated long ago, and while racism did not disappear overnight, views have evolved positively over my lifetime.

When classes began in September, my roommate and I signed up as pledges of the Lambda Chi Alpha fraternity, one of the six on campus. There were six sororities as well. At the time, you either belonged to a fraternity or you were excluded from their social activities. I really enjoyed the fraternity and became an active brother. Now, looking back, maybe I had a little too much fun. I made a lot of friends, some with whom I have kept in contact over the years. In 1996, nearly 100 of Stetson's alumni from the graduating classes of 1962 to 1972 made it back to campus for a fraternity reunion. It was fun to see how some old friends had gained weight, a few had a receding hairline, others were totally bald, and many had grown a beard. I learned at that reunion that one of the few physical attributes that does not change after puberty is the tone of your voice, which accompanies you to the grave.

I went to some fraternity parties, or, well, a lot of fraternity parties. I had a room in the main house and was involved in many activities including intramural sports, in which we competed against the other fraternities.

It was distracting, to say the least, and I lost sight of why I was at Stetson. I lost many hours of studying time partying with friends. I even played a lot of bridge, a game that I was very good at, so my brothers always wanted me as a playing partner.

My lack of focus caused me to get kicked out of school on three different occasions. The first time, I got a job selling Kirby vacuum cleaners door to door.

The first sales lesson we received was that we needed to be completely convinced that the product we were selling was the best one available in the marketplace. I bought into this hook, line, and sinker. Secondly, we should demonstrate to the potential buyer that a Kirby vacuum cleaner would leave the home cleaner than any other brand. Finally, we had to ask the potential customers to refer us to other people. I always asked my customers to refer me other potential customers.

Although times have changed, it was my observation that most housewives did not buy anything without the approval of their spouse. Therefore, I always made sure that both husband and wife were at home when I made my sales presentation.

I really enjoyed selling vacuum cleaners. Most people want their carpets, curtains, and sofas free of dirt and bugs that may transmit disease. To my advantage, my demonstration Kirby had a see-through collection chamber through which you could observe the dirt and grime being sucked into the vacuum cleaner. This was a very powerful sales tool. Later, after the presentation, I tried to identify which member of the house was more impressed by the effectiveness of the equipment I was selling. It was usually the woman, and then she would do the hard work of convincing her spouse that they should buy it, since they "cannot sleep one more night with those horrible bugs as their sleeping companions!" I sold Kirby vacuum cleaners for about six months and managed to sell quite a few. This sales experience gave me confidence to overcome shyness.

I have never understood why colleges do not offer sales technique courses to their students. Working as a salesman taught me skills that helped me become successful in life.

In my opinion, to succeed means to fulfill one's dream and not reach old age lamenting what could have been accomplished but was left undone. I believe that selling ideas should be taught in school, preferably at the university level.

With the money I saved from the Kirby job, I bought a white sports car, an MGB that had red upholstery and a black convertible top. I drove back to Stetson after my semester off in my new car, feeling like a rich kid. That semester, several fraternity brothers and I rented an apartment in Daytona Beach for spring break. Tens of thousands of college students were celebrating their Easter break, like they used to do five years earlier at the beach in Fort Lauderdale. It was now happening in Daytona. I spent practically the entire semester partying at the beach.

It did not take long before I was again removed from Stetson. This time, my oldest brother, Genaro, who worked at the Ford Motor Company in Dearborn, Michigan, got me a job in a factory where Ford's spare parts were painted. I worked there for an entire semester and much of the summer of 1966. I started working in the packaging department wrapping up the spare parts that had already been painted. I ended up working the night shift as a painter, because I was paid 20 cents more per hour. Thank God this activity did not affect my lungs. Although I used a gun to paint and wore a protective mask, the hairs in my nose were dyed red and I had paint all over me. Even so, I left Michigan very happy, because I had managed to save what for me was a fortune: $1,000.

Once again, I was accepted back by the university. Yet once again, one semester later, the partying continued and I was asked to leave the university for a third time. This time around, however, in 1968, I decided to change the course of my life and I volunteered and enlisted in the U.S. Army, one month before my 21st birthday.

6

AN OFFICER IN THE U.S. ARMY: THE VIETNAM WAR

In February 1968, I joined the U.S. Army. After signing up, my first destination was Fort Jackson in South Carolina. I was put through a series of medical, psychological, and intelligence examinations. I remember that some potential soldiers did not pass the physical tests and were happy that they got to return home and avoided the Vietnam War. I was not only found fit for duty, but I was told I was a "perfect specimen". Not to toot my own horn, but I also scored very well on the intelligence tests, so I was invited to join the Officer Candidate School (OCS) and the Flight School. I called my mother to tell her the news, and she told me that my older brother had been offered the same thing two years earlier, but he had decided to continue as an enlisted soldier. She also told me that she had nothing against my aspirations to become a U.S. Army officer, but she preferred that I did not enroll in the Flight School. I decided to heed her wishes.

Before joining OCS, I had to complete an eight-week basic training program in Fort Gordon, Georgia. Every day, they got us out of bed to line up the platoon in formation at 0600 hours. After physical training and before breakfast, we assembled again at the chow line, in which we stood, in perfect formation, to enter the mess hall. We marched daily to the same cadence, "left, right, left, right," to prepare for the parade of the graduation of the upperclassmen of our company.

It reminded me of Cuba nine years earlier, when Fidel Castro took power with a group of bearded militiamen dressed in olive green with a rosary around each of their necks, pretending they were a group of devout Catholics going around the streets of Havana. The people laughed behind their backs with their typical Cuban sense of humor and imitated the military cadence, saying, "Un, dos, tres, cuatro, comiendo mierda y gastando zapatos!" *(One, two, three, four, eating shit and wearing out shoes!).*

Fort Gordon's basic training was strenuous and very regimented. One day, the sergeant punished us by forcing us to run with our backpack, shovel, canteen, and rifle. Almost all the recruits were falling down along the way, with only three of us managing to continue to the finish. When the sergeant ordered us to stop, I asked, "Why did you stop? Are you tired?"

Thank God, after that much running, he must have thought that we had already been punished enough, and he just smiled, with a sort of friendly smirk on his face.

After successfully completing basic training, I was promoted to E-3, a rank below corporal. Although it was not much, I made more than $100 a month with housing, food, and clothing included. The next eight weeks I was stationed in Fort Dix, New Jersey, where I did more advanced training. From there, I was off to OCS, this time in Fort Belvoir, Virginia. It was a great experience. In fact, it is one of the few military experiences that I recommend to anyone who wants to know what they are made of and whether they have the backbone and stamina to withstand extreme mental, intellectual, and physical pressure. We were 120 soldiers divided into two platoons, but only 62 of us managed to finish the 23 weeks of training required to graduate as a second lieutenant of the U.S. Army.

The first order given to aspiring candidates was to drop off our duffle bags in the barracks and run in formation to the barbershop to shear off our hair. Some of the upperclassmen served as our supervisors and made sure our haircuts were short enough. If not, it was a return trip back to the barbershop. Over the next 12 weeks, the upperclassmen took turns harassing us, yelling at us, constantly bringing us down in relentless fashion. There was always someone yelling at us, and we were only to respond with our names. In my case, "Sir, Candidate Fernández, sir!"

We were to obey their order immediately. If we did not do it they were screaming in our ears, with harsh criticism. Sometimes we had five different orders that we had to obey simultaneously, which put even more pressure on us. We had to run everywhere, and if a candidate were caught walking, they had to do 25 to 50 push-ups. We had to polish our boots subject to routine inspections which subtly forced us to buy fancier boots that kept a more elegant shine. Unfortunately, it was a while before we could break in those boots, and we all got massive blisters, which were painful and lasted for weeks.

I remember that first night after our haircuts the upperclassmen forced the whole platoon to sing the American national anthem. I did not know the lyrics, so I remained silent. When they realized this, several instructors began yelling at me: "Why do you not sing, smack head?" The shouting continued, until finally, in a moment of silence, I could yell, "Sir, Candidate Fernández, sir. I am not singing because I do not know the words. I am not a U.S. citizen!"

My answer surprised all of them and for a moment no one said a word. Someone finally gave an order: "That is not a valid excuse, by tomorrow morning at 0530 hours, you will sing our national anthem in front of the platoon. They all want to hear that you are one of us."

I spent that whole night memorizing the words, and I do not have a good singing voice! I have a terrible ear for music and I know this, but I proudly got up and sang the national anthem the next morning, and despite my tone deafness, I think my superiors were pleased that I had learned the lyrics.

That night was a mere preview of what was yet to come. I did not sleep more than three hours a night during the first 10 weeks. The upper classmen took turns keeping us awake until one thirty in the morning, and before going to sleep, they would destroy our barracks, from turning over suitcases and trunks to overturning beds and chairs. They made our barracks look like a pigsty, but by 0600 hours, they had to be ready for inspection. That is, we had to pick it all up in the dark with only the help of a flashlight.

The beds had to be perfect, so much so that if you threw a quarter on it, the quarter would bounce. If it did not, the bed had to be remade. Under no circumstances were excuses accepted. A phrase that was repeated all the time was, "An excuse is not an excuse. Excuses are unacceptable." Little by little I learned and developed habits that I have now put into practice in my career as an entrepreneur and executive.

In fact, in my opinion, one of the two major diseases that harm humans is *"excusitis,"* that is, inflammation of the excuse. Years later, I read a book that I highly recommend, *The Magic of Thinking Big,* by Dr. David Schwartz, published in 1959. From it I learned that you need to remove from your vocabulary expressions like "because," "but," or "cannot." I stopped using excuses to justify failure. I replaced those words or expressions with constructive creativity, and developed a "must do" mentality. In other words thinking, finding solutions and always taking action. The other major illness I discovered in my childhood, while trying to learn to dive into a swimming pool, is *"fearitis."* That is, inflammation of fear. The fear of failure causes inaction, and most humans use destructive creativity to find justification to save their own ego before others.

The hardships of the first weeks of officer training were certainly not limited to sleepless nights and strenuous exercise. Breakfast, lunch, dinner, and every situation in between were trying moments. During meals, we were instructed to look straight ahead, with our chest out and chin in. We were never allowed to eat anything that was larger than a centimeter by a centimeter and we were never to look down at the plate. Obviously, no one could eat under those conditions. At the end of each meal, we would just drink a glass of milk and hope that was enough nutrition for the meal. Between the lack of sleep, not to mention the continuous physical exercise and difficult academic classes, many of the candidates who wished to become officers simply gave up, many of them crying.

In our platoon, the candidates took turns in leadership roles so that each one of us could be properly evaluated. After two months in the program, we had to rate our fellow surviving candidates' leadership skills from 1 to 100. This rating would represent 50 percent of our total evaluation, with the other 50 percent coming from our tactical officer, or the officer in charge of training. I learned from this experience how to be as objective as possible and to reduce one's subjectivity when evaluating another individual. The end result was not the opinion of one individual, but many people's evaluations averaged to form a group consensus. I have always applied these principles in every business I have managed with the purpose of identifying excellent workers and weeding out those who are unproductive, whether they are executives or regular employees. This system has allowed me to promote or dismiss employees in the most logical and objective manner possible.

After eight weeks, my platoon tactical officer, Robert DeLuccia, informed me that I had been evaluated number 1 in leadership. He also told me that he did not wish for the result to go to my head and he assured me that if he saw me being more relaxed, he would force me to do 100 push-ups. He was not joking. I remember one time I had a terrible muscle spasm in my back that caused me a large amount of pain, even when I was just breathing. I asked permission to go to the infirmary. His response was "Drop! Do one hundred push-ups!" As I was counting out number 75, the pain in my back disappeared.

Nevertheless, it soon seemed as though DeLuccia had it in for me, because the 100 push-ups became a frequent order. I believe this garnered sympathy from my fellow platoon members. I must admit that it was not all bad: after 23 weeks of training and graduating from OCS, my physical condition was at its peak.

I completed OCS, and was recognized as a Distinguished Military Graduate, meaning that I was among the top 10 percent of the graduating class. I was also bestowed the Leadership Award for placing first in all evaluations. I was very proud, and I was lucky that my father, still teaching at Suffield Academy, and my mother, still teaching mechanical drawing and Spanish in Fort Lauderdale, were able to take a few days off from work and attend my graduation.

We were all shocked to see my brother Genaro's father-in-law, Dr. Louis Tordella, also at the graduation. We knew he had a position in the U.S. government, but we found out that day that he was very important when my superiors asked me about my personal relationship to him. In fact, they had to take special security measures due to his attendance.

Dr. Tordella was a mathematician of Italian descent who was among a group of American military intelligence officers that deciphered German codes during World War II. Over the years, he became a senior member of the National Security Agency, an organization that is arguably of greater importance than the Central Intelligence Agency. I was so honored that he was there to place the golden bars on my uniform that symbolized my promotion to second lieutenant. He also presented me with the two awards that had been bestowed upon me, the Distinguished Military Graduate and the Leadership Award. Also present at the graduation was the commanding general of Fort Belvoir, Virginia.

Now, as a second lieutenant, I had been offered a position as a tactical officer in the same OCS. In this position, I was to train future officer candidates. During the next 12 months I supervised 120 candidates, only about half of whom would graduate. My objective was to train future officers for the Corps of Engineers and Military Intelligence of the U.S. Army, keeping in mind that almost all of these officers were going to the war in Vietnam under the pressure of real combat, in leadership positions. We were to teach them until it would stay engrained in their minds, "Say what you mean and mean what you say." We supervised their physical training and watched them while studying to be sure they were not asleep. Of course, we had to convey an impeccable image.

I remember many years ago, when we lived in Fort Lauderdale, I suggested to my father, a devout reader and educated man, that he should write a book. His response was, "Why, if everything is already written?" He believed that any topic you would like to learn about could already be found in the volumes on the shelves of a library. He knew that I was fascinated by the lives of General George S. Patton Jr. and Douglas MacArthur. I had read about them before enlisting in the Army.

Patton became a four-star general and MacArthur a five-star. Both of them dressed in a peculiar manner, but always correctly. I wished to project a similar image to General George Patton but without the ivory-handled pistols or the riding boots. I wanted to mimic the legendary, impeccable image that so many around the world had admired.

The stories of both generals' courage and leadership inspired me. At one point, during World War II, Patton presented his plan of attack, containing four battle lines: A, B, C, and D. The first line, A, was at the front, facing the enemy, and D line was at the rear. In the initial scheme, Patton was placed in line A, leading his troops, but the high command ordered him to place himself in line D. For him, it was only right to set an example for his men, but he had no choice but to obey orders and place himself where instructed. So Patton placed the D line at the front, facing the enemy.

General Patton possessed entrepreneurial savvy where there had been few in the military before like him. His quality of leadership, always side by side with his men in the toughest and most dangerous moments, and his way of thinking and behaving, truly motivated and encouraged his subordinates to fight and accomplish their mission. He was in command of the 3rd Army, always leading in the front line where you have to make many important, creative, and critical decisions. He was an extraordinary man. One of my favorite stories relates to an order from the High Command that Patton was "not to attack or take possession" of a certain city in southern France. Patton replied, "The city is already taken and in the hands of the Allies. Do you want me to give it back to the Germans?"

After graduating from OCS I was promoted to the rank of Second Lieutenant. Douglas Mallek, a former classmate from OCS, was also selected as a tactical officer and suggested that we should share an apartment in the City of Alexandria near Fort Belvoir. We were both single and he thought it would be a good idea to divide up the household expenses. We earned about $350 a month, but our bank accounts were almost empty around the 20th of each month. I remember the last days of the month I often ate lunch and dinner at the nearest McDonald's.

In October 1969, I met Nicole Lewis Cylkowski at a party at the Officers Club at Fort Belvoir. In December of that same year, we were married in the Catholic church at Georgetown University in Washington, DC. Nicole was 26 and I was 22. She had studied to be a schoolteacher at George Washington University but was working as a secretary at a law firm called Nixon, Mudge, Rose, Guthrie, Alexander, and Mitchell. The first and last names, Nixon and Mitchell, were eventually removed from the letterhead, because Richard M. Nixon was elected President of the United States in November 1968, a position he held until August 1974, and John N. Mitchell had joined the President's cabinet.

The wedding reception was held at the Officers Club at Fort McNair in Washington, DC, along the Potomac River. Of the 250 guests, more than half traveled from South Florida, although a large number of relatives and friends living in the vicinity of the capital attended. Nicole's father, Henry, a self-made entrepreneur, not only covered the wedding expenses, which is the tradition in the United States, but he also gave us a check for $10,000 that we used to pay for our wonderful honeymoon in Puerto Rico.

Soon we received news that we would become parents, but I had my marching orders to go to Vietnam. I solicited the U.S. Army to postpone my Vietnam orders until the following year, since I wanted to be present for the birth of my first-born.

That is how it happened. Alejandro Francisco was born on March 12, 1971. Six weeks later, I was deployed to Vietnam. On the way to Vietnam, I made a brief stop in San Francisco, where I visited a cousin of my father, Francisco Centurion, and then made two more stops, in Alaska and the Philippines. Then it was on to my last destination, Saigon, where I went straight to a military camp, the 90th Replacement Battalion, near Biên Hòa.

My fellow soldiers and I were assigned a cot in a tent and were told that in seven to ten days, after reviewing our records, they would send us to our next destination. In front of the briefing room there was a large hole caused by a mortar that had fallen the previous week. I thought: "What a welcome!"

I left my duffle bag next to the cot and went to the Officers Club for a beer. My beer was only half-finished when a voice came over the loudspeaker summoning a Captain Fernández. Wow, I thought, "That's me!" I went to the main office and was informed that a jeep was coming to pick me up with my destination orders. "I have only been here a few minutes," I had said, confused by the quick assignment. "Maybe there is another Captain Fernández?"

There was no other Captain Fernández and twenty minutes later I was at Engineer Command Headquarters, based in Long Bình, a very large military base. A first lieutenant introduced himself and immediately asked if I remembered him. His face looked familiar, but I could not recall his name. He had been an aspiring candidate at Fort Belvoir, and I had been his tactical officer. When he saw my name among the newcomers' records, he requested an interview.

We chatted for a few minutes and he assured me that while I had been hard on him and his classmates at OCS, I had always treated them fairly. He told me he would do the same. He offered me different posts, including a covert mission to Cambodia. I told him that it might be prudent to consider an alternative assignment. I told him: "I'll go anywhere, but a Cuban citizen in the United States Army could be quite a spectacle if captured by the Communists in Cambodia."

Days passed and the lieutenant began to worry about the need to quickly assign me to a post. At the Long Bình base, I found another lieutenant whom I had instructed at OCS. He told me more or less the same thing: I had been hard on him during his training, but he had never felt abused. He got me an interview in the same base, with a lieutenant colonel in S-4 (supplies) at the Engineer Command. He asked me if I had graduated from college as an engineer. I said no but that I was a very fast learner. He also wanted to know if I spoke Spanish, to which, of course, I said yes.

I have always believed that my guardian angel always shows up when I need him the most, and that was confirmed on this occasion. The previous post of the lieutenant colonel had been Panama, where he had learned some Spanish and did not want to lose it. He said, "You will work with Major Smith, but in the morning you will join me for coffee to chat in Spanish." From that experience I learned that when one is fair to others, the gesture boomerangs back around. We reap what we have sown, as the saying goes. I have kept this philosophy all my life and it certainly has helped me thrive. I showed both lieutenants my appreciation for what they had done for me, but, unfortunately, I have not seen them again.

At the base of Long Bình there were about 40,000 soldiers. It was like living in a small military town. My new duties were to coordinate the supply of equipment between private contractors and U.S. Army warehouses. Sometimes parts had to be ordered from the mainland in the United States, and I soon learned that it was best if the equipment were made by only one company, with the same make and model, in order to get replacement parts immediately.

However, the armed forces did the opposite. State lines and Congressional Districts influence Department of Defense appropriations. Consequently, it would not be uncommon for 10 senators from 10 different states to influence the U.S. Army to acquire its equipment from different companies. My job was to inventory all the spare parts for equipment of different brands and models, and sometimes I felt like the main character of *Mission: Impossible*.

These logistical lessons were very helpful years later when I started the TelePizza business. One of my very first decisions was that all the ovens would be from the same company and would be the same brand and model. We continued this principle on down the line even to include the technology equipment of the company and our delivery mopeds.

We were bored to death at night on the military base and many of the officers drank excessively. They drank dry martinis as if they were water and played high-stakes poker. I started out playing fixed-limit games of $10 bets, but ended up playing in no-limit games where you could bet whatever you wanted. If I won, my mind was clear and I returned the next night to play again. However, if I lost, I needed a day or two to relax before going to play again. My strategy worked, and I won three out of four nights I played, on average. Since I returned from Vietnam, I have not played poker again.

On August 25, 1971, I received a phone call at 0700 hours.

"Captain Fernández?" I heard on the other end.

"Speaking," I replied.

The voice on the other end of the line was resigned. "It is Colonel Jones. I am calling from Saigon, and I am sorry to give you bad news."

The first thing I thought was that my 81-year-old grandmother Romelia had died. But the words that followed so thoroughly shook me I had to sit down. "I regret to inform you that your mother has passed away."

Hours later, I received a telegram from my father telling me that my mother was gravely ill and asking that I return home as soon as possible.

I flew to San Francisco and, from there, to Miami. At the airport, I took a taxi to the Caballero Funeral Home on Eighth Street. My mother had died two days earlier. Her body, lying in the coffin, seemed as if she were expecting me.

The next day we buried her. It was after several hours that I was able to release all the emotions that I had kept inside since I had received the call from the colonel. I cried in the arms of my uncle Francis, my mother's eldest brother, who came to pick me up at the Greyhound bus station in Fort Lauderdale. I had not cried since the early days of my exile from Cuba.

My mother and I had made a pact before I left for Vietnam that when I returned, I would finish college. We wanted to start a construction business like the one her father had built in Cuba in 1909, after he graduated with an engineering degree from the Rensselaer Polytechnic Institute in Troy, New York. She promised me that she would get the necessary certifications for her to sign drawings as an architect in Florida.

We both felt that to achieve economic success in the business world it was necessary to open a business of our own. I said to myself that I would make every effort to follow my mother's advice and fulfill my dreams.

Ten days after the funeral, I had to return to Vietnam. A few months later, during the rest and recuperation week (R&R) the U.S. Army granted to all combat soldiers in Vietnam, I flew to Hawaii, the closest state to Vietnam, to become a U.S. citizen. This is something I had delayed for some time. I guess that deep down I thought at some point I would return to Cuba. Following in the footsteps of my father, I opted to change my surname, Fernández, to another less common last name. My 1971 U.S. passport read: Leopoldo Francisco Centurion, also known as (AKA) Leopoldo Francisco Fernández Pujals.

7

BACK TO STETSON UNIVERSITY

When I returned from Vietnam, I was accepted again at Stetson University. I knew I had not studied hard enough before and I was determined to do things differently this time. The university required that a failing grade (F) be compensated with an A and a D with a B, so I had to focus and concentrate on academics. After a long year of hard work, from 1972 to 1973, I finally graduated with a major in accounting and a minor in finance, earning mostly A's and a few B's.

Of the courses I took, two helped me the most in my future businesses: business communication, which taught me to write concise, direct letters, and cost and managerial accounting, where I learned how to calculate the sales break-even point of any enterprise.

The four years I had spent in the military had passed, and I found upon returning to Stetson that the atmosphere of the university and the fraternity had changed. It was now 1972, and the preppy look of brand-name shirts and short hair was long gone. The hippie look was in and everyone had long, unkempt hair. It had become fashionable to smoke marijuana and to use other drugs, like LSD. I had matured in the U.S. Army, and was a family man now. I stood out in contrast to the chaotic, free-spirited environment taking hold of the younger students.

When I visited my old fraternity, Lambda Chi Alpha, I did not know any of the new fraternity brothers, but some had heard of me. A few days later, I was approached and asked to get more involved and submit my nomination for High Alpha, the fraternity President. At that time, there was a clash between members who were using drugs and those who were against drug use, so, yet again, I decided to complicate my life.

I was elected President, and my first order of business was to meet with every one of the fraternity brothers on the topic of drugs. Users were in the minority, perhaps 10 percent of the chapter. My aim was to convince them that their activities could reflect poorly on the fraternity and to push it out of the house if it were to happen at all. This was sensible, and after a few months the hostility simmered down.

At the same time, I turned my attention to the physical condition of the fraternity house, which was deteriorating. I reached out to alumni in the hope of raising some money to fix and furnish our fraternity house with new rugs, drapes, and upholstery. We were successful: the image of the house improved.

Shortly after re-enrolling at Stetson my wife, Nicole, inherited about $7,000 after the death of her mother which came from the sale of her house. We used the money, along with my savings from the U.S. Army, to buy a rundown house near campus and across the street from an elementary school. I thought the house was a real bargain at $10,000. We started renovating and painting, fixing whatever was damaged, and even upgraded the landscaping. For just $1,000 (not to mention 18 months of our time and efforts) we gave the house a facelift. All the work paid off. When I graduated in 1973, we sold the house for twice what we had paid for it.

While I was in school, Nicole continued to work as a secretary for a small law firm, and I was hired as a nighttime security guard at the university. In the mornings I went to class and we left our son, Alejandro, at a daycare center. When my mother was alive, she was always on top of what her children and grandchildren were doing. After she had passed away, my father assumed that role, visiting during every vacation break from Suffield Academy and calling us every week.

Finally, after many starts and stops along the way, I graduated from Stetson University. Alejandro was already 2 years old and I felt satisfied with my accomplishments. We were ready for the next big thing and we decided to move to Tallahassee, the capital of the State of Florida, to start a business with one of my fraternity brothers, Bruce Shelfer. Our idea was to launch a nightclub and restaurant in the estate house that, supposedly, Bruce's father was going to give to him.

Tallahassee's population was about 100,000, excluding students from various universities. Nicole and I bought a house for $40,000, putting down the $20,000 we had earned selling the last house as a down payment.

Nicole returned to work as a secretary in a law firm, but soon resigned. For my part, I got a job as an accountant in the government of the State of Florida. Since I wanted to have my own business and needed additional income, I also worked as a bartender at the Roadway Inn bar to learn the trade. Later, after Nicole had left her job, I also worked two night shifts at Hardee's, a fast food restaurant.

One weekend my father visited us and announced that he had married a lady named Catherine (Kay) who previously had been a Catholic nun. She was an American of Irish descent. She was 20 years younger than my father and her maiden name was McKinley. They had met when Kay and my father were studying for a master's degree in Spanish at Trinity College in Connecticut.

For better or for worse, the nightclub never materialized. One day, Bruce's father called me and proposed to meet me at the bar of the Roadway Inn hotel. He said he was very impressed with me and that he wanted to invest in the nightclub, but he did not wish for his son to participate in the business. I thanked him, but declined the offer, as I would not have felt right accepting such an arrangement behind my friend's back.

Shortly afterwards, I met a man who sought me out as a partner in a hotdog franchise. I wanted to do due diligence and went to a few meetings with professors at the Hotel and Restaurant School of Management at Florida State University to learn more. What I learned in those few meetings opened my eyes to the opportunities offered by the fast-food industry. All of the professors agreed that it was "the future" of the restaurant industry!

This is the backyard of our home built by my grandfather Francisco Pujals' construction business in 1940. It was located on 5th Avenue at the corner of 24th Street in the Miramar neighborhood of Havana.

This is the front side of our family home in Cuba, after being stolen by the Castro regime, it is now being rented to the Philippines government as their Embassy, as can be appreciated in the photograph with the flag and shield of the Philippines.

CONSTRUCTORA PUJALS S. A.

3ª AVE. 1808 MIRAMAR. MARIANAO

ARQUITECTOS. INGENIEROS. CONTRATISTAS. HABANA. CUBA. TEL. B-8842

ING. FRANCISCO PUJALS CLARET
PRESIDENTE

ING. FRANCISCO PUJALS MEDEROS
1ª VICE PRESIDENTE

ARQ. ELENA V. PUJALS MEDEROS
2ª VICE PRESIDENTE

ARQ. ALICIA PUJALS MEDEROS
TESORERA

DR. GENARO FDEZ. CENTURION
SECRETARIO

ING. RAUL MORA S. GALBAN
ADMINISTRADOR

This is the architecturally innovative office of the Pujals Construction Company, designed by my mother and built in 1954. The Pujals Construction Company was founded in 1909 by my grandfather. In the lower right hand side of the building is the apartment rented by the Hungarian who warned my parents that communism was coming.

Photo of my father (seated) with his family, circa 1925. My grandparents Genaro Fernández Peña and Maria Dolores Centurión Maceo are standing. My aunts Olga Fernández Centurión (left) and Anais Fernández Centurión (right) are sitting next to my dad.

Abril 1958

Photograph of my maternal grandparents with their four children and their in-laws in 1958. From left to right, standing: José Pujals Mederos, Genaro Fernández Centurión, Francisco Pujals Claret, Raúl Mora Suárez Gálban and Francisco Pujals Mederos. Seated: Gloria Lizama Verdeja, Elena Pujals Mederos, Romelia Mederos Cabañas, Alicia Pujals Mederos, Mercedes Alvarez Pedroso.

With my parents, Genaro Fernández and Elena Pujals, my younger brother Eduardo in the center and my older brother Genaro Carlos on the right.

My grandfather Genaro posing on top of one his Spanish Horses outside his home near the San Ramon sugar mill, not far from the city of Manzanillo in the Oriente province. My grandfather arrived in Cuba in 1874 alone, shortly after turning 14 years of age.

The home in the village of Las Piñeras, about seven kilometers from the City of Pravia in the Asturias province of northern Spain, where my grandfather was born in 1860.

My great-grandfather Francisco Centurión Zapata, Colonel of the Spanish Army. He was born in Nerja, Málaga, in the southern part of Spain in 1845. He was assigned to Cuba when it was a Spanish colony in 1868. After retiring, he married my great-grandmother Francisca Maceo Valdés.

My great-grandmother Francisca Maceo Valdés.

Francisco Maceo Osorio, uncle of my great grandmother, born in Bayamo, Cuba. He practiced law and became one of the leaders of the Cuban Independence Movement that led to the Ten Year War (1868-1878). This was the longest of three wars before Cuba became a free and independent country.

My mother holding me in her arms when I was six months old.

My brother Genaro and I (white shirt) playing at the park in front of our home on Fifth Avenue.

With my older brother, playing cowboys at the 5th Avenue Park. I was on top of the goat that Titi, our cook, had given me as a present. We called him "El Chivo" which means "the goat".

The Havana Yacht Club, one of the world's oldest social clubs, was founded in 1868, during the time Cuba was a colony of Spain.

Diving head-first into the Havana Yacht Club swimming pool, after I learned to control my fears.

My classmates and I celebrating Carnival at the La Salle kindergarten located on 20th Street in the Miramar neighborhood of Havana.

Felicia Guerra, nicknamed Titi, our Jamaican cook of whom I have many fond memories. My father sent her assistance from exile, and I also supported her until she died. Afterwards, I have continued to help her daughter and granddaughter.

From left to right: my cousins Alicia Cristina, Maria Elena, Graciela and Isabel and my brother, Genaro Carlos. We all lived together in different homes in the family compound built by my grandfather.

Playing with my cousins Alicia Cristina and Maria Elena in their dollhouse.

With my brothers wearing the La Salle School uniform. From right to left: Genaro, Eduardo and me.

My baseball team at Suffield Academy. I am the uniformed baseball player standing in the far right.

The entrance to Centurion Hall, the classroom building I donated to Suffield Academy in memory of my father. The building is three stories in height, built into the side of a hill.

Leaning on the 1966 MGB I bought during my first years at Stetson University.

My great aunt Elena Mederos who participated in the first cabinet of Fidel Castro as Minister of Social Welfare. Later, in exile, she founded a Human Rights Organization called Of Human Rights. On the right are my brother Eduardo and Frank Calzón. Frank continued leading the organization my aunt founded.

My graduating Officer Candidate School (OCS) class at Fort Belvoir, Virginia. I am the only one smiling, far left, third row.

A photo of me as a tactical officer in charge of training in OCS at Fort Belvoir, Virginia.

My mother at the airport the day I left for Vietnam. She is
holding her first grandson, my son Alejandro.

Wearing my Captain's uniform at Long Binh Military Base, the headquarters of the Army
Corps of Engineers in Vietnam.

8

SUCCESS IN SALES AT PROCTER & GAMBLE

After having rejected the offer made by Bruce's father, the concept of starting a fast-food business would not leave my mind. It was all I could think about. When Nicole and I bought the house in Tallahassee the mortgage was approved based upon two incomes. Nicole had stopped working and suddenly I had to work three jobs to keep up with the payments. I was living on a treadmill, always in motion but never progressing. At this rate, I would never achieve my dreams of having my own business, so we decided to sell the house and move in with my father and Kay, his new wife, in Fort Lauderdale.

He had just retired from Suffield Academy and they were living in our family home. I started to look for a job in sales, because I knew I could make a fair amount of money and have a flexible schedule. I wanted to have spare time to focus on my real goal: to open a fast-food restaurant serving typical Cuban food as well as regular American hamburgers.

I had already planned it out. It would be a place similar to the last coach of a train. In America, these coaches are normally painted red and are called the caboose, so I decided to call it the Red Caboose and stick with a train theme.

It was 1975 and I was 28 years old. I interviewed with a headhunter company to help me find a job as a salesman, and shortly after, I was included in the selection process for a sales position at Procter & Gamble. For three months I went through various tests and numerous interviews, and in the end I was offered a job in the bar-soap and household cleaning products division in Broward County, Florida.

My sales territory included Fort Lauderdale, Hollywood, Dania Beach, and Pompano Beach. During the three months of the interview process, I made the most of the time and worked at a local McDonald's, learning how to operate a successful fast-food business.

A little later I found a piece of land located very close to a railroad track, which I thought was perfect because of its location, size and asking price. Along with my aunt Alicia, an architect like my mother, I began to work on the design of the Red Caboose. At the same time, I registered a company with the State of Florida. With the architectural drawings in hand, I visited every Cuban doctor that I knew in Broward County and showed them the blueprints of the building and the pro forma business plan, attempting to persuade them to invest $1,000 to $2,000 in the business that I wanted to start up. For the doctors' peace of mind, the money was deposited into an escrow account controlled by a lawyer. When I presented the plans to build the Red Caboose to the construction companies, the lowest quoted price was $90,000 plus equipment. I had sold 49 percent of the shares of the company to the doctors for $40,000, so in order to not lose the majority in the business, I would have to ask for more money to make up the same percentage. I did not have enough courage to approach them again, so I realized that my dream would have to wait a little longer. I returned their money and continued dreaming.

In November 1974, shortly after I had been hired, I took a sales course in Cincinnati, Ohio, home of the Procter & Gamble headquarters. The course lasted a week, and when I returned home, I remember feeling more motivated than ever to do my job and to meet my objectives. Sales courses have always helped me with new ideas and motivated me for continual development. There were three key ways to earn commissions at Procter & Gamble. First, of course, you had to meet your individual sales targets. Second, it was necessary to attain the objectives of the geographic area in which you worked, all of South Florida in my case. Last but not least, you needed to meet the budget set by both the supervisor and his boss, that is, to meet the budget for the whole State of Florida. The company's aim was a 10 percent sales increase over the previous year, not counting the price increases due to inflation. My results were, quite frankly, spectacular. By the end of March I had already achieved 100 percent of my annual goals. My boss could not believe it. The head of the Southeast and the Vice President of sales came from Cincinnati to Fort Lauderdale to visit me. They wanted to know where and how I had gotten such outstanding results.

When I told this to my father, he told me that in Havana during the early 1920s the American directors of the International Telephone & Telegraph

Corporation (ITT) showed up one day and asked for "Mister Alcasssarrr". Actually they were there to meet Juan Alcazar, my father's uncle who was head of the Yellow Pages division of the Cuban Telephone Company, which was a subsidiary of ITT. The yellow pages used to show a financial loss for the telephone companies and when the Yellow Pages suddenly started generating a profit, the executives wanted to know how my great-uncle had managed to do so. Apparently, he was the first entrepreneurial executive who sold advertising in the yellow pages telephone directories.

Now, returning to the meeting with the Procter & Gamble executives from Cincinnati, the first thing they asked was if I made sales outside of my territory. Of course, I said no. I explained to them that the purchasing manager of the drugstore chain Super X, where our products were sold, almost never met with salesmen. After two weeks of communicating with the buyer's secretary, I changed my approach and appealed to her on a more personal basis. I told her that I had just returned from the war in Vietnam, I had just graduated from Stetson University, and that I was new to this job. I asked her to help me get an interview with her boss, and bingo! The woman decided to help me. She told me that her boss was a very disciplined and hardworking man, and that he had expressly requested that she not arrange any interviews or meetings that he had not asked for. However, she tipped me off that he was, in addition to being Purchasing Manager, the head of the Marketing Department for the southeast region. While I had no chance of seeing him during the week, she confided that he came to the office every Saturday at 7 AM to clean up his desk and organize himself for the following week without any interruptions. This would be my chance!

The next Saturday I got up at 5 AM and was in the parking lot of the Super X's headquarters at 6 AM. Sure enough, just as she had told me, a car arrived at 7 AM and a man got out and strode with a sense of purpose toward the office doors. I approached him and introduced myself. I asked for five minutes to explain an idea that would be of interest to him, because it would increase sales and profits at each Super X store.

My entrepreneurial mindset captured his attention and little did he know I was using a technique I had learned in sales training: to sell the sizzle and not the steak!

I explained that at that very moment my company was offering a promotion on cleaning products, with a 15 percent discount on purchases of a minimum number of cases. At the same time, the Super X chain could benefit from free television advertising of his stores, provided that Procter & Gamble products were exclusively included in the commercial. It was a win-win situation for everybody.

The specific product was not at the forefront of the sales presentation: discounts, profits and free television commercials were! When you sell the sizzle, the customer asks loudly for grilled meat.

Furthermore, when you present the purchasing manager ideas that increase his profits and they turn out to be true, he will see you as a partner and a friend. In short, the head of the marketing and purchasing departments of Super X drugstores for South Florida loved the idea and continued with the rotation of products on television commercials in subsequent months. I had become his buddy.

The Procter & Gamble executives were finally convinced that I did not sell products outside of my territory. My first-quarter sales exceeded 100 percent of the annual budget, so they raised my monthly salary from $900 to $1,000! I was promised that at the end of the year, if the entire area met their target, I could get a bonus of 10 percent of my annual salary. Not only did I fulfill my sales objectives in three months, but I doubled them in six months and tripled them in seven.

At the same time that I was enjoying some early success in sales, Nicole was not working outside of the house. Our expenses were minimal, since we lived in my father's house, and she looked after little Alejandro.

She began to tire of my idea of starting a business and thought I was living in a dream world. The Red Caboose required more than double the original planned investment, so after I returned the money to our investors I kept working at Procter & Gamble for a few more months. Nevertheless, I had reached the conclusion that Procter & Gamble was not the right company for me at this point in my career. I told Nicole I would find a better position elsewhere and would succeed with another multinational company.

When I told my father, he looked at me like I was crazy and asked, "Why would you stop milking this cow with all the milk that it has given you?"

In general, human beings settle into comfort zones and rarely strive to achieve their dreams. Normally, people who surround you and who love you will advise you based on what they think or how they behave.

From experience I know that the majority of those who are not entrepreneurs try to discourage those who wish to have their own business. They are not aware that this is creating a mental block that stops many potential entrepreneurs from achieving their dreams.

9

MY BEGINNINGS AT JOHNSON & JOHNSON

Companies like Johnson & Johnson, IBM, and Xerox were searching for qualified salesmen with a minimum of two years of successful sales experience. My time at Procter & Gamble, which was one of the best schools for selling, meant that I was a very attractive candidate, but I had only worked as a salesman for nine months. Through the headhunter that had previously helped me search for a job as a salesman, I got an interview with the southeastern regional manager of Codman & Shurtleff, Inc.

Codman was a wholly owned subsidiary of Johnson & Johnson, which sold surgical instruments and medical devices. The selection process was long, similar to the three months I had experienced with Procter & Gamble. During my first interview, they were skeptical about hiring me because of the two-year sales track record requirement.

I turned to one of the sales techniques that I had learned and I asked the executive interviewing me, "Are you looking for someone with two years of experience or someone who knows how to sell and has an exceptional track record of increasing the sales of his company?"

"What do you mean?" he asked. I could tell I had his attention.

"In four months at Procter and Gamble I exceeded 100 percent of my annual quota in sales," I told him.

He laughed in disbelief and dismissed my assertion. "That is impossible!" he said.

Undeterred, I put into practice another tactic I knew to be useful in overcoming objections, including skepticism: to arrive at a pre-agreement. "If I prove it, would you reconsider your decision and offer me a job as a salesman?"

He accepted. Having made our agreement we decided to meet again the following week. I gathered the sales reports from Procter & Gamble that demonstrated my performance. The computer printout reflected year-to-date sales compared to the previous year, but could not show percentages of four digits. Since my results exceeded 999 percent, asterisks accompanied the figures. For three of our products my sales exceeded 1,000 percent of the goal, and all categories and products were above 100 percent of the prior year.

Faced with the evidence, he could not help but wonder how I had achieved it. I explained my strategies and he told me that he would recommend me for an interview. Two weeks later, I was interviewed by the company's Vice President of Sales, who lived near Boston. When the executive arrived at the Fort Lauderdale office, he wanted to meet with me immediately.

He got straight to the point: he asked me to describe myself in a single word. In a heartbeat I replied, "catalyst."

When he asked why I had chosen that word, I replied that, "Just like in a chemistry laboratory in which a catalyst causes a reaction, my concerns, energy, and creativity had the same effect of provoking positive and constructive reactions." That is still true to this day.

The interview became friendlier and we engaged in a light-heartened banter at the end of which, he offered me a job. I started on August 15, 1975. I was assigned to the State of New York, covering large medical centers from Albany to Buffalo.

Prior to starting, I had to be trained for the job in Hartford, Connecticut. Upon arriving in that city I contacted my trainer, Robert Barnoski. Bob had two years of experience and was eager to be promoted to management, because he wanted to be a product manager. He was surprised that I called him on a Sunday night, and I proposed a breakfast meeting the next day at the hotel where I was staying.

Bob was an American of Polish descent, three years younger than me, and had graduated with an engineering degree. At breakfast he described his journey with the company, the products he sold, the hospitals he visited, and what my training would consist of. Every afternoon I had homework assignments to complete in the evening.

I studied anatomy, congenital diseases, and even surgical procedures. In the morning we visited the hospital operating rooms in his area, and I could see that his enthusiasm and dedication were remarkable. Bob was a good salesman. I learned very quickly and even made suggestions to him to improve his results. He taught me everything about the surgical instruments and equipment that we sold, and I studied the technical materials of the course for hours and hours at night.

As I said, we had a good relationship. I dared to teach him some sales techniques that were second nature to me. Bob accepted my suggestions very willingly. We started by applying one of the lessons I had learned in Officer Candidate School, the 5 P's: Prior Planning Prevents Poor Performances. Before entering a hospital we analyzed the information that we had about each department, which instruments were bought from other companies, and which new products we could offer. At Procter and Gamble I was taught that one of the first steps of any sale is identifying or creating the need. By asking questions and sometimes even appearing naïve, we got department heads to tell us about their needs and the problems that they wanted us to help them solve. Without much effort, we were achieving sale after sale. Bob realized immediately the importance of identifying and/or creating a need before selling a product.

I remember one hospital in particular, one of the largest in the area, where Bob had not managed to sell anything. The head nurse would not even agree to meet with him, nor with any other salesperson. I advised him to use empathy, and Bob asked me what that was. "Put yourself in her shoes," I told him. We thought hard about the purpose of a visit, which was to sell the repair services of the surgical instruments that we offered, which were superb. But the real problem was that we had to get our foot in the door!

I told Bob that women loved attention and flattery, and I hatched an ingenious plan. Bob demurred nervously that it was not according to his personality and in any case, would never work in a million years. Nonetheless, that afternoon, Bob called a florist and ordered a dozen yellow roses for the hospital operating room supervisor. He instructed that they had to be delivered at 8:30 AM, and the bouquet included a friendly but urgent note asking her to meet with him that very afternoon, because he wanted to introduce her to a foreign executive who was visiting the city.

Bingo! The supervisor was flattered and felt honored so she agreed to meet us that day. Of course, the foreign executive was me (which was technically true). After introductions I started to ask some naïve, carefully calculated questions. Even though we assured her that we would take little of her time, we spent more than an hour and a half with her, and at the end we came out with an order to repair more than 20 surgical instruments. This helped Bob break the ice and create an opportunity for future sales.

Shortly after, we had a visit from Wayne Knupp, regional sales director, who was our direct boss. He invited us to dinner, during which he offered me the sales territory of Manhattan and Northern Jersey, which were under his area of responsibility. The previous salesman had been promoted to product manager at the parent company and he needed to fill the vacancy as quickly as possible.

I had assumed I got this theoretically more important territory, Manhattan, because Bob had spoken highly of me. However, over dinner a week earlier he confessed to me that he had been offered the position and had turned it down. The hospitals in Manhattan were big, important hospitals with prestigious surgeons operating there. However, Bob explained to me that to earn good bonuses and commissions it was better to work in areas of steady population growth. For this reason, nobody wanted Manhattan. Prestige aside, it had a population growth of virtually nothing.

In front of our boss, I decided to put Bob in a tight spot. "Bob, you were offered that territory and you turned it down. Why?" I asked.

Bob blushed and stuttered until, smiling, I told him I was joking with him. Then, addressing our boss, I said, "I decided to work for this company because I abandoned the idea of starting my own business and I promised my wife I would devote myself, body and soul, to what the company asked of me. If the company wants me to work in Manhattan, I shall do so."

The following week I finished my training and went to Danbury, Connecticut, to an apartment that we had rented, where Nicole and Alejandro were waiting for me. The following Monday I drove down to New York City and met with Glenn, the salesman of the territory. He was about six foot six, with red hair and carried a little extra weight on this tall frame. Glenn took me to the hospitals in the area and introduced me to the people responsible for each department. Out of the 30 hospitals we visited, we only met with four purchasing managers and two surgical operating room supervisors. All the other people occupying key positions did not meet with us, and I quickly noticed that the copies of the sales invoices were not even filed properly. His sales had been stagnant for over a year, and I did not understand how it was possible that he had been promoted to product manager. It was one of the first surprises of my corporate career: if this salesman had been properly supervised most likely he would have been fired. Instead, he had gotten a promotion. I assumed that he would occupy a chair at the company headquarters and exemplify the Peter Principle, which states, "In large corporations and bureaucracies, employees are promoted to their level of incompetence." Said another way, the selection of a candidate is based upon their performance in a current role, not the envisioned role. Thus, they stop being promoted only when they fail.

There is a very distinctive case that I frequently use when I teach management training courses. I like to observe that Pan American taught the world how to fly and then went bankrupt.

The first thing I did when I started working in Manhattan was establish a little order to the chaos. When I got home each night, I devoted myself to organizing the invoices that Glenn had left unsorted or filed without any rhyme or reason (such as by hospital or by date). Acquiring in-depth knowledge of what each hospital had purchased allowed me to identify key opportunities, an essential step in the sales process.

I also decided to improve and increase my knowledge in the surgical area. I decided to be at the hospitals each morning as early as possible, in order to observe as many surgeries as possible. Thanks to the direct dialogue with surgeons and nurses, I not only learned to identify their needs, but I got to establish relationships that were of great help in the short, medium, and long term.

I had to increase sales. I was not about to come up with an excuse for failure. My only options were to increase sales or, alternatively, to increase sales.

Since I had inherited a bunch of closed doors in just about every hospital, it was virtually impossible to meet with the operating room supervisors who were the key decision makers. I decided that every night I would write letters to each one that I had tried to visit, explaining what Codman & Shurtleff could offer. After receiving three, four, and in some cases even 10 of my notes, many recipients were curious to get to know me. Eventually they all began to grant me interviews during my weekly or biweekly sales calls.

However, the great increase took place from January 1976 onward. Part of this was because I had sent a personalized family photo Christmas Card to each operating room supervisor. I believe that once they saw a human face and a real family behind the person who wrote so many weekly or bi-weekly notes, they developed an interest in meeting me personally.

One of the best habits I learned in my time in the U.S. Army is that "Perseverance is essential to fulfill the mission. Never forget that accomplishing the mission is the most important thing." My observation is that it is very easy for people to throw in the towel before fulfilling the mission.

In one memorable instance, I met with an operating room supervisor who had not met me previously. Her fiancee worked for Weck, a surgical instrument company that was Codman & Shurtleff's biggest competitor in New York City.

She told me that she had only agreed to meet with me because she was curious to meet the person who had demonstrated such perseverance and tenacity. She told me straight away she was about to get married and that she had to buy everything from Weck, so I did not need to visit her again.

Fortunately, I was well versed in our products and knew everything that Weck offered in its catalog. So I congratulated her and immediately shifted gears to identify a disposable product that was not in Weck's catalog. I knew that most nurses in operating rooms preferred disposable products whenever possible to eliminate cleaning and sterilization work. I knew Weck did not have a disposable vein stripper, so I asked her what the hospital was using in surgeries to remove the saphenous vein in varicose vein surgeries.

As I expected, she told me they were using Weck's traditional product which was not disposable. This would be an easy sale because we offered a superior disposable version. I had identified a need, and I closed the sale by asking, "If Weck had a sterile disposable product that you could send directly to pathology, not worry about losing any parts of the instrument and which did not require sterilization, would you buy it from your fiancée?"

Of course, the answer was yes, but she told me they did not have such a product. I told her that I understood what she had said just a moment ago and that she could not buy anything from me. Nevertheless, I said that I would like to give her a gift of a disposable vein stripper made by my company. I explained its advantages and left the free sample with her.

A week later an order came through from her for an entire box. She allowed me to keep visiting her and, after each encounter, she would buy some additional products. It almost became a game to find things her husband's catalog did not have. This was like picking up nickels and dimes: all small numbers, but it was fun.

In any case the game did not last too long because two months after the wedding, they separated, so she began to buy all kinds of products from me. That hospital ended up being one of my best customers, because the supervisor helped me contact the heads of other departments. I am paraphrasing Pablo Picasso, who said, "When inspiration arrives, one should be busy working." This is a lesson that you should always be selling and you should behave correctly because you never know what the future may hold.

Another strategy I implemented was to clearly identify the easiest products to introduce in each hospital. Ideally, a product had to be disposable or require periodic service so that it generated repeat business. I designed a matrix, so that I could have a bird's-eye view of my yearly objectives at each hospital. In one column,

I would write the names of the hospitals and the most important departments. In successive columns I wrote the products I was interested in introducing. This overview highlighted the new products that I had introduced into each hospital and reflected my progress in each operating room in my territory.

I have to admit my results were excellent. My monthly commissions exceeded my fixed salary, and I calculated that at year-end, I could reach $30,000, a significant figure at the time. I had tripled my income in about a year.

Then I heard through the grapevine that the manager responsible for the Latin America territory had left the company, so I decided to apply for that position. Not surprisingly Wayne Knupp, who remained my direct superior, did not want me to leave his area of responsibility. However, during my initial interview to join the company, I had communicated to the Vice President of Sales my wish for an international position. He promised me that I could move to the International Division after I had proven that I could sell the full range of products in the domestic market. I had demonstrated success, so I insisted that Mr. Knupp intervene and organize the interview with the Director of the International Division of Codman & Shurtleff.

A month later, finally, we got to meet each other. He accompanied me one morning as we went from hospital to hospital, and that was enough for him to offer me the job in his area. Meanwhile, I had to train my successor and teach him everything I knew about each hospital, including the people he should meet. I found out that my substitute did quite well for a year, but then I lost track of him.

As time passed, I realized that my knowledge and my self-confidence had increased. My father kept sending me books, now about sales, through which I learned many important things. I captured the experiences and teachings of the best salesmen that had been in the United States up until then, through books such as Dale Carnegie's *How to Win Friends and Influence People,* Frank Bettger's *How I Raised Myself from Failure to Success in Selling,* Joe Girand's *13 Essential Rules of Selling,* and Og Mandino's *The Greatest Salesman in the World.*

10

FROM SALESMAN TO MANAGER

We had moved to Braintree, near Boston, Massachusetts, and I was working in the head office of Codman & Shurtleff, Inc. I felt that I was on the right track to becoming a senior person in the multinational company Johnson & Johnson. Nicole, Alejandro and I were happy with the move to the headquarters of the company. We felt it was a great opportunity. I liked my career and I embodied the saying, "Doing something you enjoy is never a chore."

If I continued as the salesman in my Manhattan territory, I would have made what I then considered a fair amount of money: $30,000 per year: $12,000 in fixed salary and $18,000 in commissions. If I got the sales manager job responsible for Latin America, my total income would be reduced to only $20,000 fixed salary plus a 10 percent bonus. A good salesperson can earn a lot of money, but sometimes you have to take one step back in order to take two steps forward. So, I decided the glass was half full: my fixed salary had increased from $12,000 to $20,000 and the package included an office and a secretary.

It was 1976, and Alejandro was now 5 years old and only spoke English. I wanted him to learn Spanish, but he only knew a few words, like numbers from one to 10. Despite the fact that I would soon start to work in the international division, we were still living in the United States, and my goal was to relocate to a Spanish-speaking country.

When I was traveling, Nicole would visit her father in Connecticut. My father-in-law, Henry, had sold his business and devoted all his time to his new home, built on approximately 100 acres on the outskirts of Hartford. He had remarried a woman of Polish descent, who, despite three generations of her family having lived in America, still spoke Polish at home.

The first thing I had to do in my new job was analyze sales by country, distributors, and products. My immediate boss, the executive who had interviewed me a few months earlier in New York, traveled constantly to Europe, the Middle East, Australia and several countries in Asia. Sales grew steadily, and every country of any significance was buying our products. Among the smaller countries, Costa Rica was the one that stood out because it purchased more products than the rest of Central America combined.

Analyzing the prices of each product in the international price list, I noticed that my boss, probably because of a lack of knowledge or interest, barely took the time to examine the computerized data. One thing that stood out was the profit margins were the same for all of our products – a straight line gross margin of 60%. A better approach was to charge more for some and less for others based on the product exclusivity and market conditions. So I created a price list similar to the one we had for the domestic market. In this process I noticed that the prices of our products that had no competition were very low. Their gross margins were too low, so I decided to increase some of them. Shockingly, the opposite was true of products for which we did have competition. I decided to lower the prices of competitive products up to 20 percent. These were our "bread and butter" items for which there could have been great demand.

Finally I ran some numbers comparing the previous year's sales with the estimated revenues based upon the new pricing that I was going to propose. The result of my projections showed total sales would increase 35 percent and gross margins would increase an astounding 200 percent!

My boss and I had long discussions on this issue, to the point that he asked me if I was out to get his job. His attitude really surprised me. He was insecure to the point of having a complex!

Unfortunately, I have found a number of instances of this nature throughout my professional career. From that moment on, our relationship became quite difficult. He consulted the Vice President of Marketing for the domestic market with the intention of killing the price list I was proposing, but to his great surprise the VP endorsed my proposal and agreed to the price list that I suggested. Sales, gross margin, and the value of the International Division of Codman & Shurtleff rose substantially after the implementation of the price list that I had recommended.

My job also required me to travel around the country to attend international surgical congresses. I visited cities such as San Francisco, Chicago, Las Vegas, and New Orleans. At these meetings I met many surgeons from Mexico, Panama, Venezuela, Brazil, Argentina, and Chile, amongst others. I spoke with them in Spanish and sometimes I acted as a translator, a task that left me exhausted. All those contacts helped me to open up new markets. For instance, Dr. Mauro Loyo Varela, from Mexico City, later became the President of the World Congress of Neurological Surgeons and was particularly helpful to me. We have maintained a good friendship over the years.

Another strategy I used to increase sales was to visit the Johnson & Johnson Managing Directors in each country to find out who were the best distributors in each particular country. During one of those visits, the Managing Director responsible for Central America and Panama informed me that they were looking for someone to lead the region's medical surgical division.

When we said goodbye, the General Manager told me that I should not be surprised to receive a call from New Brunswick, New Jersey, where the company had its headquarters, to be interviewed and to discuss the possibility of moving to Central America.

During the months I was in charge of sales for Codman in Latin America, I struck up a friendship with Peter Webster. He was General Manager of the factory in New Jersey where the needle holders sold in our catalog were made. In my opinion they were the best in the world. Peter was extremely dissatisfied with his boss and told me that he would be interested in going into business for himself and setting up a factory in Mexico. Mexico had closed the country to imports of all the products that were manufactured there, and such a factory would definitely have been a success.

Peter was an engineer who liked adventure and loved Mexico. He spoke fluent Spanish. He wanted to open the business with me. I mentioned the project to a number of Mexican surgeons, many of whom showed a clear interest in investing in the business. Nevertheless, our discussions with Peter did not go any further.

As had been predicted, my boss received a call from the Vice President of Johnson & Johnson's Latin American Division requesting to interview me for an executive position in Guatemala. The role was for marketing all of Johnson & Johnson's medical and surgical products in Central America and Panama. My boss asked me about the origin of this request and wanted to know if it had been me who had asked for the interview. I had not asked for it directly, but it struck me as humorous that a few months earlier he had been restless thinking I was interested in his job. Now he was upset because he feared being left alone!

The following week I went to the Johnson & Johnson headquarters in New Brunswick, New Jersey. I had read a book by John T. Molloy called Dress for Success, and I knew that the appropriate attire for that interview was a navy-blue suit, white shirt, burgundy tie and shined black shoes. As my father said, dressing up always leaves a good impression. I met with an executive named Antonio Forlenza, who was about 65 years old, and rumored to be retiring. The interview started with general questions about the work that I was doing at that time, how long I had worked at Johnson & Johnson and the position I had held the previous year. Then he described the profile of the person they were looking for. At one point, he excused himself, got up from the chair and left the office on the pretext of carrying out a consultation. When he came back he told me that in his opinion, I did not have the appropriate experience.

It was the second time in my career I had received such a response, but I knew how to handle it. Directly and without hesitation, I asked him, "Are you looking for someone with experience or someone who has an incredible track record of success?"

I paused for a slight second and then continued, "During this year, sales in my area have increased by 100 percent. The same thing happened last year in Manhattan. During the time I worked for Procter & Gamble, I tripled sales in just seven months. If we go further back, to my time in the U.S. Army's Corps of Engineers, you will see that I won the Leadership Award and graduated among the top 10 percent of my class as a Distinguished Military Graduate in the Officer Candidate School. You may find someone older than me who has more years of experience, but none with a successful track record similar to mine. I learn fast and I get results. If you give me a chance, you will not be disappointed."

He remained silent for a few seconds, which seemed like an eternity. As I had learned in these selling situations, "He who speaks first loses," so I kept quiet.

Suddenly, he apologized again and left the office. I guess he went to tell his boss that he was wrong because when he returned, he said, "You convinced me. The position is yours."

Once again I realized how important it is to know how to sell an idea with conviction in order to open doors. I remember that I returned home happy and satisfied. There is nothing in the world that can compare with a well-executed sales presentation.

11

A Promotion and Transfer to Guatemala
with Johnson & Johnson

On July 3, 1977, Nicole, Alejandro, and I traveled to Guatemala. Before boarding the airplane, a few nostalgic thoughts ran through my mind, including the Red Caboose project in Florida and the surgical needle-holder factory in Mexico.

Both were great ideas, but did not become reality, as it was not the right time. Great opportunities only work if taken on at the appropriate moment. To detect that perfect moment you must be able to analyze the potential, ensure you have the necessary resources, implement strategies and act without a single doubt to obtain results. In other words, it is essential to focus mind, body, and soul on the enterprise.

When I arrived in Guatemala, I found that the salesmen of the medical and surgical division were not properly selling but were merely "order takers". This included the product manager and the person I was going to replace.

The only college graduate was the sales manager. Although he was not bilingual, eventually I was able to teach him how to sell. Years later, I heard that he left the company to start his own business.

Division Managers like me were required to attend frequent regional Latin American meetings. In one of those meetings I met a Cuban-born American citizen, named Marcos Perez. Marcos, along with his boss had managed to restructure and turnaround the Ethicon Sutures Division in São José dos Campos, Brazil. Afterwards, he was promoted to director of the Hospital Products Division to repeat a similar task: reorganize it and turn it around.

Marcos gave me a brief but immensely useful lesson, saying: "When I started as the right-hand man of the director in the Ethicon Sutures Division we took a photo of all the sales and marketing staff. With the photo in hand, we identified the worst salesmen, who represented about 10 percent of the total number of employees. In 60 days, they were all dismissed and we hired and trained their substitutes."

He continued: "In the photo we placed an X on those who were replaced and during the following two months we continued in the same manner, identifying the low performers. It took two years to clean up the division of employees who did not have the right profile to perform this type of work."

When my father, as always, asked me about the activity that I was performing at the time, I told him that my most important task was to select a new team of salesmen. Those were magic words to my father. Ten days later, I received five new books by five authors who were experts in how to conduct interviews or how to make the right decisions when hiring personnel. I read each of them with great interest and tried to implement techniques on how to search for the right people who could become good salesmen and future executives of the company. Interestingly, I learned about the technique that had been used on me years earlier, by reading one of these books. The book suggested taking it a little further. So, in interviews I requested that a candidate define him or herself with a single word. Then, I would ask what word or phrase their parents would use to define them. By using this tactic I was able to understand different points of view about the candidate and it also gave them an opportunity to explain their responses and convey how he or she thought others saw him or her. Another question I liked to ask each candidate involved solving a math problem that was challenging but solvable quickly with logic: "What is the product of 13 x 13?"

On more than one occasion candidates told me they needed a calculator, to which I firmly replied that I did not need to hire a calculator. The purpose of my question was not only to find out their mathematical ability, but also to detect what level of effort each person would put forth in order to solve a problem. To get to know their level of honesty and ethics, I also asked them what they would do if someone walking in front of them reached in their pocket to remove a handkerchief and a ten dollar bill fell out onto the sidewalk. Would they return it or put in their pocket? I learned a lot from the candidates answers about their manner of thinking and ethics.

We implemented a strategy to hire university graduates who were bilingual in Spanish and English, as this was a necessity for working at a multinational company in Guatemala. We would put ads in the newspaper, which said, "Multinational company wishes to interview college graduates, bilingual in English and Spanish, who want to pursue a professional career."

Training and replacing the staff was not easy. We ultimately replaced the entire sales team with the exception of the sales supervisor. After a year, the sales and marketing team was increasing sales and introducing new products in the marketplace like they had never done before.

At the time we were undertaking these changes we hit significant headwinds with the Managing Director of Central America and Panama. He came from the North American consumer division. There, the effort in sales was focused on the effectiveness of television advertising, and salesmen were mere "order takers". In this way the company avoided having to pay high salaries to its salesforce.

It took a while, but I finally convinced him that sales had to be made face-to-face and that a college education was an essential qualification, even though salespersons with a degree commanded a higher salary. While we had our differences, I have to say that the Managing Director was a good man and a devout Mormon. He loved to run every day and got me into running, too. After a year, I returned to excellent physical condition, very similar to when I was at the Officer Candidate School. As my boss heavily favored the consumer division, he sometimes made bad decisions that affected my area in a negative manner. Our differences boiled over to the point that I decided to leave the company. To my surprise, Johnson & Johnson fired him when they learned of my resignation. To replace him, they brought in Antonio de Reguero, a Venezuelan who had been the Managing Director of Johnson & Johnson, Ecuador.

Antonio was persuasive and convinced me that I should stay in the company. I rescinded my resignation and continued putting all my efforts into turning the division around. In three years we tripled sales, taking the division from red numbers into the black with profits that represented more than 10 percent of net sales.

I want to emphasize here that many people fail when they are promoted because they do not learn to make the transition from employee to manager or from salesperson to sales supervisor. As discussed previously, this is known as the Peter Principle.

In my professional career I have observed many times that companies put all their effort into teaching employees when they start working. After performing their duties for a while, when they have become the best, they are usually promoted. Inexplicably, the companies do not usually teach them how to develop in their new roles. They are not taught how to manage people, properly select personnel, develop and motivate subordinates, evaluate them, and fire or promote them.

It is necessary to know how to do these things so that the people under your supervision perform their jobs and are ethical, efficient, effective, and disciplined. Sometimes you have to do some handholding and explain clearly what your subordinates have to do.

After receiving the appropriate training and support, if that employee does not carry out his or her work, it indicates that there is a problem of attitude or aptitude. The boss has to detect and weed out the bad apples. This cannot be delegated.

In such situations, the first rule I follow is to give clear notice of the problem. If the employee does not react and still does not perform his or her duties well, he or she will be given a second notice. The third notice is to allow him or her to leave the company. At that time I explain to the employee that they will be happier and better suited for work at another company.

This is something that many managers do not do well. I frequently say that you can lead a donkey to water, but you cannot force it to drink. Telling an employee to find other work is something almost all executives postpone. In such cases, fear is in charge and always accompanied by all kinds of excuses. *Excusitis* and *fearitis* really are diseases. Unfortunately, there are many executives suffering from these two illnesses. In my opinion, this is because they have not received adequate training and they make two critical mistakes of judgment. First, they do not understand that by protecting an ill-suited employee they are putting the livelihoods of others in jeopardy. Likewise, they fail to understand that employees really are better off in a job they perform well.

I have always tried to convey to those who work with me that it is essential to select good people. "If you surround yourself with stars, you will shine, and if you surround yourself with mud you will get muddy." At the same time, it is essential that the boss becomes the guide or teacher and provides moral support to each member of the team under him or her.

After living 17 years in the United States, the way I expressed myself was seen as pretty peculiar in Guatemala. For every four words that I spoke, one was in English. To solve the problem and recover my forgotten vocabulary, I asked my father to send me books written in Spanish. He did not send fiction. As always, the books had to do with learning new sales techniques, self-development, how to interview personnel and management. To help me, my father visited an old acquaintance whom he called Günther. He was the former Managing Director of the Bayer Company in Cuba and had retired in Palm Beach, Florida. My father told him about my previous job at Procter & Gamble and my current job at Johnson & Johnson and asked him to recommend books specializing in management. Günther's response was very clear. "In the 1940s and '50s, the people that did not read books written by Peter Drucker lived virtually in ignorance."

My father found all the books published by Drucker, some in English, some in Spanish, some with yellowing pages bought in secondhand bookshops. These books became my main reading material over the following months. The main book of Drucker's, which I define as the bible for executives, is *Management, Tasks, Responsibilities and Practices.* I read one book a week, and it did not take much time to enhance my managerial knowledge.

There is no doubt that there is a cure for every disease, but first you have to identify it and then act in order to resolve it. I am of the opinion that in school it should be encouraged to teach techniques of self-training, so that students become autodidactic, in order to solve problems.

While in Guatemala City, we lived in two houses. The first was in Zone 14 near the international airport. The second was in Zone 9 near the Spanish Embassy. We enrolled 6-year-old Alejandro at the American school. From the beginning he stood out as a well-behaved student with noble character, good values and a passion for being a good friend.

My father and Kay came to visit us in our first home. Although my father knew it was a developing country, the question of just how developing led to one the first impressions my father had of Guatemala. Our joyous rendezvous almost ended in tragedy when my father fell into a manhole in the middle of a residential street. Thieves had removed circular iron plates that acted as manhole covers over city sewers. This left a huge hole in the middle of the road. Almost like the scene from a movie, my poor father was walking through our neighborhood and looked toward the sky after hearing the sound of an airplane. In one step he fell almost 10 feet down a manhole, but somehow survived in one piece. As Kay was caring for him, my father, would joke: "Guatemala is no longer a developing country, it is an underdeveloped country!"

During the years I lived in Central America, between 1977 and 1980, Guatemala was not safe. It was especially unsafe for foreigners working for multinational companies. Kidnappings were common and financed the communist guerillas. On January 30, 1980, the Spanish embassy, which was just one city block away from our home, was invaded and taken over by communist guerillas.

The police fired shots and a cloud of smoke swallowed the area. Nicole was at home alone with our younger son, Carlos, who had been born in Guatemala just a year and a half before. Nicole called me in a panic, scared to death, asking what to do. I told her to bolt the doors, stay away from the windows, and to lie down on the floor with our baby.

Fortunately, Nicole and Carlos were fine, but 36 people died that day. This terrible, scary situation made Johnson & Johnson take action. They sent a former CIA agent as a consultant to teach us different techniques to avoid being kidnapped. As 'reassuring' as CIA training can be, the best protective measure was moving to Panama, where we could live in a safe country without the constant threat of guerilla kidnappings. We did just that in April, 1980.

That same year, Antonio de Reguero, Managing Director of Johnson & Johnson in Central America was promoted to President of Johnson & Johnson, Spain, a much larger market. An Australian who did not speak a word of Spanish replaced him in Panama. He came from the Gillette Company and everything was new for him. I have positive memories of him, but we worked together for just a short time because I had other job offers.

One of these was for a new position at Johnson & Johnson, Mexico, as director of the Ethicon Sutures Division, which had gross revenues of $8 million a year. I seriously debated accepting the position. Even though I knew the country and many Mexican doctors well, the poverty and pollution in Mexico City, combined with my lack of confidence in the Managing Director made me hesitate in accepting the job offer.

In the end I decided not to accept it, and for a few more months we continued to live in Panama. My decision was influenced by a call from Marvin Woodall, international Vice President of Critikon Inc., a wholly owned subsidiary of Johnson & Johnson that had recently been created and specialized in the intensive-care market in America.

Mr. Woodall was looking for a bilingual manager with a college degree and sales experience. The ideal candidate should have been successful in recruiting and training other bilingual university graduates for sales positions. Mr. Woodall had interviewed four candidates in Spain, with no success whatsoever. In reality, there was only one person with such a profile in the entire company.

Mr. De Reguero informed him that the person he was looking for was in Panama, and his name was Leopoldo Francisco Centurion.

12

ARRIVAL IN THE MOTHERLAND

It was now 1981 and I had never been to Europe. Since we left Cuba, we never had the means to make a long, expensive trip. All the money that my parents earned they invested in providing a college education for their three children. The job offer in the Critikon Division in Spain interested me enormously. Finally, I would be able to live in what we Cubans call "The Motherland", Spain.

I have always had a high opinion of Spain and Spanish culture, even if my father would sometimes call the country Cuba's "stepmother" due to the friendly and favorable treatment the Spanish government gave Castro's communist dictatorship.

The interview process for the position in Spain was similar to my previous ones. However, this time it was unnecessary to sell my résumé. My successful track record spoke for itself, and there were many Johnson & Johnson executives who had already vouched for me.

I traveled to the Johnson & Johnson headquarters in New Brunswick, New Jersey, to be interviewed by Mr. Woodall. Above all, he wanted to know if I knew Spanish. He relaxed when I told him that Spanish was my native language. I explained to him that my accent was a little different in the same way that a British English accent is different from accents in various parts of the United States.

He was also interested in my personal life, my interests, and how I would overcome challenges. He asked if my family wanted to live in Spain and I answered that at the moment, yes, they did. We finished the interview and Mr. Woodall confirmed that he would formally recommend my transfer to Spain. There, I would start a new division with all the challenges and opportunities that would entail. Creating a new business entity from scratch had always been a dream for me and I was about to make it come true.

After our furniture and belongings were packed by the moving company, Nicole and the children spent some time in Connecticut with her father. During that time I traveled with Mr. Woodall, visiting the European countries where Critikon had offices, where we listened to the Managing Directors present their marketing plans and budgets for the next fiscal year, 1982.

We visited London, Paris, Rome, and Hamburg. All my thoughts were focused on learning the maximum amount possible. I think that during those two weeks in our European tour, I learned the equivalent of an MBA in marketing and finance. I am fond of telling people who inquire about my education that I have a college degree from the University of Life and an MBA from the School of Hard Knocks.

A degree is a signifier of achievement, but *education* is really about acquiring knowledge and applying it. Lack of a formal degree should never stop any person from learning, applying knowledge and accomplishing objectives.

In Paris, I remember we stayed at the Hotel Maurice. One morning, we were picked up and traveled down a narrow street, wide enough for only one car. We had to stop because a bread delivery truck had stopped and blocked the street. I was in the back seat and immediately opened the car door and got out. I walked up the sidewalk about 30 feet and waited. When the truck started moving out of our way, I returned to the car. Mr. Woodall was surprised and he asked me the reason for my behavior. I explained, "It is a reaction from when I was in Vietnam. I try never to get caught at a dead end street like a sitting duck." He asked no further questions.

Once my family joined me in Madrid, we settled for a few weeks in the Eurobuilding Aparthotel, where we waited for our furniture to arrive from the United States. Nicole and I decided to enroll Alejandro, who was 10 years old then, at the American School of Madrid. He quickly adapted to the new environment and, by chance, met my mother's second cousin Luis Baralt Mederos.

Luis and his family were staying in the same hotel under circumstances very similar to ours. Alejandro and Luis' son rode the school bus together and became friends. When Luis learned that his son had met Alejandro Centurion, son of a Cuban, he saw the possibility of a family connection. I received a phone call from Luis and when I told him who my parents were, he instantly placed me. He felt very attached to my family, concluding that his mother and my grandmother shared the same DNA. They were daughters of two Mederos brothers who had married two Cabañas sisters. Although later we saw each other only a few times, there were many things we had in common, especially when discussing our shared dream of a democratic Cuba.

By now little Carlos was 3 years old. We enrolled him in a Montessori school in the Montecillos development in Húmera, Madrid. We had recently found a house there to rent that met all of our needs. In the house, our staff included a lady from Guatemala who had been with our family for a few years. She had come with us to Panama and then on to Spain. The children spoke Spanish with her, though we generally spoke English at home.

Once we were settled in our new life in Madrid, I focused on achieving results in the Critikon Division, where there was a lot to do. It was an operational entity independent of Johnson & Johnson, Spain, although legally it remained under the company's umbrella. One of the first decisions I made was to recruit a financial director, Miguel A. Arcones, who in turn hired Josefina Rueda, an accountant, and Luisa Rodriguez an accounting assistant. For sales, I hired Rosa Carmona, a young bilingual university graduate, and Carlos Gomez, an electronics engineer, responsible for the repairs of the monitors that we were introducing into the Spanish market.

We began by analyzing the sales of two of the flagship products of the hospitals division of Johnson & Johnson, Spain. One of them was an intravenous catheter and the other was a machine that allowed you to control the administration of fluids to patients intravenously (IV).

After the initial hires, I quickly went to work on recruiting the sales team. I started with nine sales representatives who were responsible for covering the totality of Spain. Each one would be responsible for 30 hospitals. Each hospital had to have a minimum of 150 beds and four operating rooms and their corresponding intensive-care units. Meanwhile, I would support the sales supervisor, Gerardo Fernández, who had already worked with me in Central America.

I wish to highlight at this point that one of my rules of thumb in the management and supervision of subordinates has always been that the ideal number of people who can or should report to an executive is between five and eight. It should not be more than five employees if they are inexperienced or need a lot of supervision and monitoring. It is not desirable to have a vertical and costly structure. On the other hand, if the employees execute their tasks reasonably well the boss of the team could have up to eight people under his or her command. It should be no more than this because a great deal of time is needed to work together and motivate each employee. The idea behind the design of a company's structure is for it to be as much of a flat pyramid as possible.

It was the first time that an executive at Johnson & Johnson, Spain had taken up the challenge of hiring nine bilingual professionals with a college degree who were willing to carry a sales bag from hospital to hospital. I used the same strategy that I had used in Central America and Panama, placing an advertisement in major newspapers in the country. It read "A fast-growing Division of Johnson & Johnson wishes to interview college graduates, male or female, bilingual in English and Spanish, who wish to make a career."

We received hundreds of résumés, and Gerardo and I read them all. We selected applicants for an initial interview. From these we determined who to invite to two communications courses. In reality, the communications courses were actually sales courses that we would teach as a competitive interview. We selected the best candidates based on how they mastered the techniques. The candidates did not know anything about selling but would spend three days learning how to sell in a very natural and spontaneous way.

Word soon spread throughout all of Johnson & Johnson that the newly hired sales representatives were bilingual and had far superior academic qualifications compared to any other division's employees, including even their division directors and sales supervisors! When someone accomplishes something no one else has done before, others emulate it and their accomplishment quickly becomes the standard. This was true when Roger Bannister accomplished the previously impossible feat of running a mile in less than four minutes, in 1954. In the years following, this became a standard mile time for top competitors. This phenomenon happened at Johnson & Johnson which quickly adopted a college graduate sales force, one of the first of its kind in Spain.

Gerardo and I shared geographical areas and began to teach the new hires how to work to be productive and successful. At the beginning it is very important to accompany them on their sales calls, to ensure that they achieve success in closing sales. It is very important for their self-esteem to rise, so that they can begin to sell unaccompanied.

Learning good sales techniques allowed them to overcome their fear, which is essential for success, both as a seller and as an entrepreneur. How to practice the five P's (Prior Planning Prevents Poor Performance) was the first lesson I tried to instill in each new salesperson. I also taught them how important it was for them to know the products that they would introduce into each hospital. They developed ways to achieve the sales, i.e. the "what" and "how" to have clear objectives and strategies.

At the same time, all of our staff needed to understand the product function and be able to identify the specific needs of each public hospital. This was necessary to introduce, for example, intravenous catheters, which were one of the division's most important products. We had to design a strategy that I named "ant work." It was to convince the departments' supervisors that the Jelco catheter, which was the one we sold, was better than Abbott's Abbocath. Abbott was our main competitor and their product was so ubiquitous its name "Abbocath" became synonymous with "intravenous catheters". Nurses would literally say "order an Abbocath" the same way they said "band aid" for bandages or "aspirin" for pain killer. This was true even though the prices for our products were very similar and Jelco was the superior product.

Each salesperson had a demonstration kit that they used to present the product to supervisors and head nurses. Nurses preferred a catheter that did minimal damage when penetrating the patient's skin and that administered the maximum amount of fluid into the vein. Our product tore less skin upon insertion, caused less pain and had far greater throughput than Abbocath.

In a hospital of 1,000 beds and 15 operating rooms, we had to convince some 80 professionals. We would ask them to sign a letter, addressed to the purchasing manager of the health center, requesting the acquisition of our Jelco catheter. It was not an easy job, and it took us several months, but with the right strategy, the necessary patience, and a lot of perseverance, we achieved the objectives we had set.

Mr. Woodall had told me that in the next two years, Critikon, Inc. would acquire other companies in order to have a full range of intensive-care products to offer the Spanish market.

What neither he nor anyone in the company could have imagined was that a crazy employee of Tylenol, a subsidiary of Johnson & Johnson, would taint several capsules with cyanide and cause the death of ten U.S. citizens. Such a tragedy would have led to the ruin of many companies, but Johnson & Johnson handled the situation with distinction. Johnson & Johnson spent more than half a billion dollars removing all capsules from the market. Tylenol was reintroduced a few months later with new packaging that prevented manipulation of the product in the package.

Although Johnson & Johnson accepted responsibility and acted proactively to reassure its customers, the financial impact was serious. The scandal affected the company as a whole. The new acquisitions that were planned did not happen and the Critikon Division did not succeed as an independent division, as had been planned.

The most important part of this stage of my career was learning to compete against an established leading brand in the hospital environment. In our case, our main competitor, Abbocath, was first in the marketplace. I came to realize that in order to create a strong brand it was essential to be *first in the mind of the consumer.*

An essential quality in a salesperson is the ability to think strategically to overcome obstacles and to use his or her imagination to create the appropriate action plan. A salesperson must be creative, but above all must have perseverance and be constant: repeating the action plan over and over again.

As I learned in the U.S. Army, an excuse is not an excuse and the head of a team has a greater responsibility to teach, motivate, and strategize. All that I learned at that time served me enormously in my professional career. People management, i.e. how to inspire employees and instill the necessary desire to exceed their own expectations became one of my management specialties.

Another product that we offered in our division was an oxygen sensor for anesthesia machines, called Oxycheck. This machine monitored oxygen levels in the anesthesia machines and could not only prevent the death of a patient, but the adverse effects caused by oxygen deprivation on the brain. Although later it would become standard in all anesthesia machines, the monitor that we offered was the only one on the market at that time and it was not that expensive, at 100,000 pesetas, considering the benefits it offered. After we started selling the product, we were only able to sell 15 units in three years, and those purchases were always because the anesthesiologist requesting it had gone through the heartbreak of losing a patient due to lack of oxygen. This is an example of how cash strapped Spanish government-funded hospital budgets were at this time. Here was a product that could save lives, and it was not widely adopted.

Another product category was volumetric infusions pumps, otherwise known as IV pumps. We found that it was easy to introduce the devices that allowed nurses and doctors to set and administer the correct dosage of IV fluid. However, we had to be creative, because we quickly realized that hospitals again did not have capital equipment budgets, but rather, budgeted funds for disposable products. We overcame this objection by loaning the machine to the hospital in exchange for their purchase of the disposable supplies that could only work with our pumps. In this way we achieved a dramatic increase in sales.

In addition, we offered another enormously useful device that had excellent acceptance by hospitals around the country. It was the Dinamap, a highly sensitive and effective blood pressure monitor that worked in situations more archaic solutions could not. Despite its price of 400,000 pesetas, it was essential for heart attack and stroke treatment and we sold around 400 monitors in just three years.

The company's original plan was to convert the Critikon Division to the market leader of intensive-care products in Spain. Unfortunately, due to the tragedy at Tylenol, Johnson & Johnson could not complete its planned investment in purchasing other companies that would have enabled the division to become the market leader. I told my boss that, in my opinion, Critikon products should be integrated into the hospitals division of Johnson & Johnson, Spain in order to reduce overhead costs and make it profitable. That is exactly what happened.

13

A SALESMAN OF IDEAS: THE CENTRAL ZONE PROJECT

Shortly before the Critikon Division became part of the hospital division, I wrote a 19-page letter to Marvin Woodall, in which I explained that Johnson & Johnson as a company was poorly structured in its professional (hospital targeted) businesses.

The company had three clearly defined business areas: consumer, professional and pharmaceutical. In the letter I stated that since its inception in 1887, Johnson & Johnson's Professional Division had grown substantially, but argued that it was inexplicably comprised of 17 totally independent companies which sold their products to hospitals through their sales teams with no coordination between them.

To demonstrate the inefficiency of this system, I observed that every time a new company was purchased by Johnson & Johnson, the manufacturing, distribution, and sales remained independent. It was a totally decentralized system. High-level executives did not realize that the company was structured around the factories and not around the customer.

The Peter Drucker books had taught me that one of the responsibilities of senior management was to structure companies in such a way that they are not only effective but also efficient, without ever forgetting that the customer is the most important element. That is why I always suggest that the employees of a company be focused on serving their customers. I also think that the management system should be organized in such a way that the managers actually work for their employees, since the most important worker of a company is the one closest to the customer. The personnel must always turn its face toward the client and its back to the boss.

In 1983, I contracted hepatitis after eating bad oysters. I was quite sick, to say the least, and was hospitalized for a week at the Fundación Jiménez Díaz Hospital. Even after I was released, I was too weak to return to the office. It was weeks before I was back on my feet.

Even though I was sick, I was still working on bettering myself. I took that time to devour the books on business management that my father was still sending me, reading one per week. I remember that during my stay in the hospital, Mr. Woodall came to visit me and brought me a book as a gift. It was *Megatrends*, by John Naisbitt. I did not tell him that I had already read it, but the fact was that I knew it almost by heart. Still, I was touched by his visit.

The letter that I wrote to Mr. Woodall did not fall on deaf ears and, in fact, I had many serious discussions with him about it. "How dare you question the structure of a company that has a track record of more than 100 successful years!" he declared. Another time, he asked: "Do you really think that this company, which has a transatlantic architecture, will change direction to go in the path that you suggest?"

They were long debates and sometimes intense clashes. My boss, who had been at Johnson & Johnson for 30 years, had never met a subordinate capable of making a suggestion that was beyond his area of responsibility. That is why he did not want to convey my ideas to the appropriate level, because at the beginning they were not properly assimilated by him.

The process took several months, because my proposal had to reach the highest level of the company, the executives on the global Board of Directors of Johnson & Johnson. Mr. Woodall finally understood the value of my proposal and helped open the doors for me to submit it to the Vice President, who was responsible for Southern Europe and who reported directly to an executive who was also a member of the Board of Directors. I outlined my idea in the Johnson & Johnson, Spain conference room in Arganda del Rey, Madrid, in front of some senior executives. Present in the room were the Vice President for Southern Europe, Wayne Nelson; the President of Johnson & Johnson, Spain, Antonio de Reguero; and my boss, Marvin Woodall.

The thesis of my proposal was that Johnson & Johnson was incorrectly structured around factories, rather than focused on the customer. From my point of view, the company was incorrectly decentralized. It was effective but not efficient. Yes, Johnson & Johnson had increased sales and profits every quarter. "So why change?" my boss asked. I explained that productivity and profitability would increase even more if my proposal were implemented. Yet the key questions were "yes" or "no" and "by how much?".

The Vice President for Europe was the only one at that meeting who was on my side. In fact, if my plans were carried out, my boss would lose his job. Antonio de Reguero was only concerned about the bottom line of the profit and loss statement of his area of responsibility. Plus, he knew that if they gave me free rein of the medical and surgical divisions, the severance pay to replace salesmen, supervisors, and division directors would adversely affect him. Luckily, the Vice President of Johnson & Johnson had a different outlook, and Spain was in his area of responsibility. In addition, at the highest levels of the corporation they were already contemplating similar changes in the company structure, but not the same one that I had proposed.

At most companies there are no communication policies that allow employees to express their complaints and give suggestions up the chain of command. Most companies think that each employee can communicate with the Human Resources department, but it usually does not engage properly in these matters. What most do not understand is that the immediate superior or the boss of the employee should be addressing employee concerns without their having to wait for somebody else to solve the problem.

That is why at my company, TelePizza, I implemented the "ascending communication policy," which allows each employee to request a meeting with their boss and even the boss of their boss to voice any complaint or suggestion not previously resolved. That meeting should take place a maximum of two days after having raised the issue.

If the issue remains unresolved or the suggestion unheeded, the employee could then ask to speak with the next person up in the hierarchy, and then the next, and so on, and ultimately could reach the President of the company. The Human Resources department is in charge of ensuring that this policy is executed properly and that there will never be negative repercussions for the employees. This strategy allows thousands of good ideas to be heard in the correct place and by the right people. It also helps to detect a number of incompetent bosses, who can be either trained or dismissed.

At the Johnson & Johnson meeting, it was very curious to observe the behavior of some of the executives present. It seemed as if there was a culture of lambs following their shepherds. Everyone took on the attitude and opinion of whoever had the most authority in any given meeting. It was like the old adage: *some go to war to kill and others to dodge bullets.* At the highest levels of multinational companies where salaries, bonuses and stock options exceed millions of dollars, most executives do not want to rock the boat.

It is true that I had extra knowledge because I read the books that my father had sent to me. I had started as a salesman, and my experience had taught me how to evaluate situations from many points of view. Unfortunately, there are many executives who have based their their careers on flattery and maintaining the status quo with their bosses, reaching senior positions without proper preparation.

The proposed changes had to be approved by the global Board of Directors. For this process, I was invited to the main conference room in New Brunswick, New Jersey, and we met with Marvin Woodall (my boss), Alfred Hoffman Jr., (a member of the Board of Directors and right hand man of the Chairman James E. Burke), and Wayne Nelson, the Vice President of Southern Europe.

My presentation lasted about 25 minutes, but the subsequent discussion extended the meeting to an hour. Mr. Hoffman ultimately approved my proposal and directed the other executives to implement it. All products of the various medical and surgical divisions in Spain would fall under me in the province of Madrid and the four surrounding it (Toledo, Segovia, Ávila, and Cuenca). This was known as the "Center Zone".

I was to have a two-year period in which to prove my proposed sales department structure and the soundness of my theory. If results compared favorably to the rest of Spain, the system would be implemented throughout the country. Spain would then be used as the model for the rest of the world if the results continued as I expected them to be.

While I was in the United States, there were some people in Critikon back in Spain who were disloyal. When I returned to Spain and found out, they were dismissed because disloyalty must be "rewarded". I then merged the Critikon Division staff with the hospital division and took control of the Madrid Center Zone. I grouped the salesmen of the Critikon, Ethicon, Ortho Diagnostics, and Hospital Divisions under one roof. However, the President of the Company in Spain, Antonio de Reguero, did not allow me to fire any salesmen from the Center Zone. His argument, which I called an excuse, was that the quality of the salesmen should be the same in the Center Zone as it was in the rest of Spain. We both knew his real agenda was avoiding severance payments.

Despite everything, I went to work immediately. I conducted several sales courses, dividing the salesmen into two groups: those who performed inventory control and service, and those that would engage in increasing sales through the introduction of new products in hospitals.

In Spain in the mid-'80s, almost everybody smoked a lot of cigarettes, myself included, so I used an analogy to explain my sales strategy: If you sell Winston cigarettes and your customer already smokes that brand, you will find it easier to sell and pick up his order, but if you are selling Marlboro cigarettes, you will have to spend much more time with the customer to get him to change brands and buy the one you sell. The problem is that it is not easy to find the time to simultaneously maintain your current sales and introduce new products.

The best salesmen (who came with me from Critikon) were responsible for introducing new products, while the weaker ones picked up orders of products that had already been introduced in hospitals.

The professional relationship between a surgeon and a salesperson, when the latter is a college graduate, tends to be very dynamic. Such a salesperson could come into the operating room to observe surgical procedures, detect the surgeon's unmet needs, and then propose products that would be of benefit to the patients. Knowing the advantages of what they were selling, along with a climate of mutual respect, made it easier to sell the products. We began with the ones we considered easiest to sell and as a personal relationship developed with a specific surgeon, presented other products to him. It was not necessary to explain that the products came from different Johnson & Johnson companies.

In order to introduce the surgical material in a hospital, we sought a consensus among the surgeons. We assigned more than one salesperson to each hospital and "distributed" the surgeons among them to help build consensus. This was another project involving "ant work."

Since I had been responsible for the Medical-Surgical Division at Johnson & Johnson in Central America and Panama, I knew which products were consumed in large quantities, were easiest to sell, and which had the best gross margins. So we focused on introducing those that would most improve our bottom line.

It was good that our offices were in a separate part of the building as an unfriendly competitive atmosphere existed between the Center Zone and the rest of Spain. The directors of the other divisions were aware that if my project were successful and I were given the responsibility of the whole country their jobs would be in jeopardy. They were not only rooting against us, but fought us tooth and nail.

At the end of the first year, the sales of the Center Zone increased 25 percent over the previous year, while sales for the rest of Spain increased only 15 percent. What was more significant was the difference in profit increases. Since we had concentrated our sales efforts on products with a greater margin we had more profits before taxes: 45 percent in the Center Zone versus 25 percent in the rest of the country. We began the next year with great enthusiasm and optimism. The salespeople were convinced that with the new working arrangement they would be able to penetrate more and more hospitals and introduce new products.

We were blazing a trail, when suddenly my whole world changed, almost in an instant. Alfred Hoffman Jr., the member of the global Johnson & Johnson Board of Directors that had championed my proposal retired in the middle of the second year. Antonio de Reguero's boss, Wayne Nelson, also resigned and was replaced by a new Vice President for Southern Europe, whose professional background was in finance. Almost at the same time, Antonio de Reguero left the presidency of Johnson & Johnson in Spain to start his own car rental business. Suddenly, the project champions who had approved my project disappeared.

This resulted in the strangest situation in my career. Three months after his arrival, the new President of the company in Spain called me into his office and told me that he had analyzed the Center Zone's results against the rest of Spain and concluded that it was a big success. To my great surprise, he also told me that he had decided not to promote me to oversee the other directors because he knew that I would fire them! Even more surprising, he had decided to promote one of the executives who opposed my project to lead it.

It hit me like a ton of bricks. I felt like I had just invented the light bulb, proving against all odds that I could illuminate the city – and that an executive from the candle factory was brought in to implement my idea!

While the results were undeniable, an executive opposed to my vision was promoted so that the project would die on the vine.

It was the same situation I had experienced in Cuba at the La Salle School when I won the bicycle race and the prize was awarded to somebody else. There is something fundamentally unfair about rewarding someone for the work of another person. It was deeply disturbing to me both as an employee and as a manager that inertia could suffocate initiatives that add to the value of the enterprise.

It occurred to me that this must happen all the time – that opportunities and ideas like mine must emerge in every company only to be resisted by complacent, biased managers in those cases, too.

That is the genesis of why I decided to implement the ascending communication policy in my enterprises. More importantly, this turn of events clarified for me that I had no choice but to wean myself from Johnson & Johnson and the corporate environment. It was time to challenge myself and go out on my own.

Every day for several months I repeated to myself, over and over again, "I will not be buried without opening my own business."

14

IN SEARCH OF NEW BUSINESSES

My experience at Johnson & Johnson, along with others from my childhood in Cuba taught me a big lesson: most human beings are driven by self-interest, regardless of whether it is just and right.

It was the middle of 1986 and I was 39 years old. I took to heart stories my mother had told me long before about her grandfather Leopoldo Mederos Cabañas who returned to Cuba in 1898 after living a life of exile in Key West for more than 12 years. At age 40 with a $5,000 loan (about $140,000.00 today), he started his own business.

By the time he died, he had turned that relatively small amount into a fortune for his family. He was a self-made millionaire, back when a million dollars was an astonishing fortune. Now, at that same age, I went from being a Company Man to a man who dreamed of becoming an entrepreneur. I did not even know what type of business I wanted to open. One thing I knew was that I would not feel right competing against Johnson & Johnson, a company that had offered me wonderful opportunities.

Since the day I had started with Johnson & Johnson, in 1975, from Fort Lauderdale to New York, Boston, Guatemala, Panama and on to Spain, almost 14 years of my life and many challenges and opportunities had come and gone. Time flies when you enter with wholehearted enthusiasm into a business project, whether it is your own or somebody else's.

I ended my involvement in the implementation of the new sales structure at Johnson & Johnson in Spain. On the one hand, I did not want anyone to accuse me of undermining the project, and on the other I was also conscious of the fact that there would be clashes between me and the person promoted to complete the project. Better to prevent now what you may regret later. So, I accepted a position at Johnson & Johnson, Spain in the professional products division as the head of a department that launched products and sought new opportunities.

I started the position with a new mentality. For the first time in my career at Johnson & Johnson, I arrived at work at the official start time and went home the moment I completed my eight hours. I met my assigned schedule, nothing more. My dream was no longer to succeed and grow at Johnson & Johnson. Now, I was totally focused on my dream: starting a business of my own.

I think it is important to emphasize that one of the virtues of Johnson & Johnson is that for more than 100 years the company had grown continuously without abandoning the hundreds of small businesses that are part of the conglomerate. These are legally constituted companies or divisions that fall under the umbrella of Johnson & Johnson. They are well targeted in the health and hygiene sector worldwide. As mentioned earlier in this book, Johnson & Johnson is divided into three main businesses. One division is dedicated to selling products designed for the final consumer (such as baby shampoo and bandages), which are primarily promoted through television advertisements. A second division, the original part of the company founded in 1886, is dedicated to producing dressings for surgical operations. The third division is Johnson & Johnson's pharmaceutical business.

One of the companies in the Pharmaceutical Division grew so much that a magazine article referred to Johnson & Johnson as J & J & J, the last J being Janssen, a pharmaceutical company founded in Belgium by Dr. Paul Janssen. He never presided over his own company. He was director of research and development, which was his specialty.

The first product line I got for Johnson & Johnson, Spain was that of the subsidiary, Codman & Shurtleff Inc., the company with which I had started my activities in the United States in 1975. To prepare an executive to run this business, I chose one of the salesmen that began in Critikon in early 1982, Alfredo Martinez. I sent him to the United States to be trained at the parent company, to improve his English, and learn all about the company's range of products.

Throughout 1986, I attended several international surgical specialty congresses to identify products that we could introduce in the Spanish market. As a result of those trips I found, for example, the bovine bones of the Surgibone Company. The new products division became the distributor in Spain. In addition, Johnson & Johnson bought a company that had some very innovative disposable contact lenses, called Acuvue, which would soon become a household name. I was commissioned to do market research prior to its launch. I was also assigned to the marketing and selling of the best intraocular lens on the market, from the company I-O-Lab, a subsidiary of Johnson & Johnson. The lenses were used to replace the eye lens in cataract surgery.

That same year, Nicole and I started divorce proceedings, after 17 years of marriage. Looking back, I think our separation was a result of my intense dedication to Johnson & Johnson for more than a decade. I decided to move into a small apartment and I spent all my free time, usually after 5pm and on weekends, defining my future business.

I felt that the time had come, and I needed to regain my enthusiasm before becoming absorbed in a new project. I started with the idea of raising sheep, but after speaking with about 40 shepherds, I came to the conclusion that they knew little of the business and that their work was limited to guiding and protecting the sheep by following the instructions of the livestock owner.

Shortly after, my younger brother, Eduardo, who worked at Banco Exterior de España in Miami, sent me a *Wall Street Journal* article titled "Pizza Wars." I immediately realized that this was a business that I could undertake on my own, so I started to search for all available information about three of the world's largest pizza chains: Pizza Hut, Domino's Pizza, and Little Caesar's.

Pizza Hut had opened its first store in 1958 in Wichita, Kansas, and in 1986 already had more than 6,000 restaurants worldwide, although it did not have home delivery and did not offer discounts.

Domino's Pizza also opened its first store in 1958, in the city of Ann Arbor, Michigan, and was based on a very different operating model: it only offered home delivery and did not have seats for eating in. It also did not offer discounts. In 1986 it had 4,000 shops.

The first Little Caesar's store opened in 1959 in Garden City, a suburb of Detroit, Michigan, and had 2,500 establishments in 1986. It focused exclusively on takeaway. It did not offer home delivery, did not have seats in the shops and the only discount offered was two pizzas for the price of one. However, the customer had to go to pick up their pizzas and take them home.

I quickly realized that I could start a pizzeria and could combine the three concepts. I would offer delivery at the standard price and for customers who dined in or did takeaway, I would offer two pizzas for the price of one. I did a market survey, and the respondents said that before ordering a pizza by phone, they would like to visit the establishment to check it out and to verify the cleanliness of the kitchen. So, if everything was to their liking, they would order the pizza at the restaurant and if there were tables and chairs, they would eat it there. As always, it was a matter of listening to the customer, and I came to the conclusion that in my first shop the kitchen should be visible to the public, perhaps situated behind a large glass window facing the street. The restaurant would have a small area with tables and chairs and I would offer a discount of two for one for the customers who came to the premises.

I remained at Johnson & Johnson, Spain until December 1988. Until then, I balanced my energy and attention between my job, planning my first pizzeria and visiting my children, whom I saw whenever I could. They lived with their mother in Villafranca del Castillo, north of Madrid. They were still studying at the American School nearby. Lots of things were happening at the same time, but I was prepared to work tirelessly to make my dreams come true.

15

MY FIRST PIZZERIA: PIZZA PHONE

My first objective was to find the proper location for the first pizza store. The pilot store would be called Pizza Phone. One afternoon it occurred to me that it could be a good idea to bring in a number of past and current associates from Johnson & Johnson on board as shareholders, with the thought that each one had something special to contribute to the business.

There was Graciela, a salesperson, and her husband, Daniel, an architect who enjoyed cooking, as well as Miguel Ángel Arcones and Josefina Rueda, finance and accounting specialists who could help me with the accounting of the business, and Luis de Andés and Jaime Moliner, salesmen who were working with me at Johnson & Johnson.

Graciela and Daniel really helped me initially with the pizza preparation. Together we developed a wonderful margherita pizza. I always say, "Pizza is not fattening; only those who eat it gain weight." I have to admit that my waistline increased considerably during this time period of my life.

I learned that to produce a tasty pizza we had to ensure that the yeast fermented the dough adequately. Once this took place at room temperature, we were able to prepare the pizza. At this point, the pizza maker could stretch it and add the tomato sauce, cheese, and other ingredients, before putting the pizza pie in the oven. In addition, I discovered that it was necessary to bake pizza at a temperature close to 550 degrees Fahrenheit, much higher than the capacity of regular household ovens. The ideal amount of time for cooking the pizza was 5 minutes and 50 seconds. I would have to wait until the construction of the store was completed before I would have a commercial oven and could develop the final formula: the one that became famous with the slogan "The Secret is in the Dough."

City administrators required a smoke exhaust system in order for opening permits to be granted at a location, which required a 20-inch-diameter pipe to go all the way up to the roof of the building. Very few buildings had these exhaust pipes. At first, the locations we found exceeded our budget. We did not find any property for less than 60,000 euros. Finally, I decided to focus our search on the Pilar neighborhood, a very populated area in Madrid with plenty of high-rise buildings 10 to 12 floors high. On Melchor Fernández Almagro Street, near the Vaguada, I found the perfect spot to rent, a two-story building with 500 square feet on each floor. This was ideal for installing the required smoke exhaust system. The owners were asking for a monthly rent of 360 euros. However, the deal was made sweeter when I negotiated a two-year option to purchase the property for 12,000 euros. As with most real estate at that time, property values were increasing substantially year to year, so it was smart business to have a set-in-stone option to purchase the property for a set price. Two years later we bought the building.

I continued working at Johnson & Johnson Monday through Friday, 9 to 5. The distribution agreement I reached with the owner of Surgibone was one of the last commitments that I had initiated. These bovine bones were mainly used by orthopedic surgeons and neurosurgeons. The sales were increasing very quickly. Eventually the owner of the company wanted me to become his sole distributor, which I will further explain later in the chapter. Another product under my area of responsibility was Accuvue disposable contact lenses. As I mentioned, I was responsible for performing a market test before launching the product. In developing the strategies to launch the Acuvue contact lenses, there were many different opinions, some contradictory with one another. Launching the product successfully would have required all of my efforts, and I was ready to leave the company.

I left Johnson & Johnson at the right time. I went from managing a business with a few, but very large customers responsible for a significant percentage of total sales, to managing a business with thousands of customers each representing a small percentage of total sales. Frankly, I prefer the latter.

In November 1987 I opened my first pizza restaurant, Pizza Phone. We chose the name because one of the partners thought it sounded more American than TelePizza. When we were choosing a name for the pizza store, I was the only one who preferred TelePizza.

One of the partners who was going to supervise the shop decided to abandon the project overnight, but my guardian angel came to my aid once again. One of the salesmen who was a shareholder in Pizza Phone, Luis de Andrés, told me that his father had just been fired from the company where he had been working for the last 25 years.

My mother used to say, "good opportunities come rarely in life" and suddenly I found myself in such a situation. The following day I asked Luis if his father would be willing to work at the pizzeria, and despite the fact that he had never been in one or eaten a pizza, he agreed to meet me at the Pizza King store on Orense Street. There, on the spot, after he recovered from his initial surprise, he accepted the job offer. I told him that his work schedule would be from ten in the morning to six in the evening. At 5:30 pm, I would arrive for the evening shift.

I remember it was then that I made the wise decision to stop smoking. I was 40 years old and I decided the time had come. The truth is that I used to cough a lot each morning and I was conscious that the task ahead of me would require plenty of energy. It was necessary to improve the breathing capacity of my lungs, and I knew quitting was the right thing to do.

I stopped cold turkey. As Benjamin Franklin said when he was young, "if an architect is able to visualize a building and then draw it so that others were able to build it, then every person should be able to dream whatever he wants to fulfill his objectives in the short, medium, and long term." I visualized a better life, and then built it.

Franklin also realized that our vices, or bad habits, are the main obstacles to reaching our goals. He thought that, in order to eradicate a vice, or bad habit, it was necessary to develop a virtue, or a good habit, to replace it. He hit the nail on the head, because when we decide to acquire good habits instead of fighting the bad ones, the latter will be forgotten without us even realizing it.

In his autobiography Franklin wrote about 12 vices that he wanted to correct and identified virtues with which to replace them. He concentrated on one virtue per week, and he self-evaluated and analyzed his behavior on a daily basis. After 12 weeks, he would start all over again.

This perseverance and self-determination led Franklin to feel so perfect that, without realizing it, he had adopted a rather arrogant and dogmatic attitude toward his friends. They began to reject his behavior by distancing themselves from him. He decided to right this situation by adding another virtue to the list: humility.

The personal and professional development of Benjamin Franklin was so inspiring and he was held in such esteem that Philadelphia, the city in which he lived, was chosen to host the meetings of the Continental Congress. There, the representatives deliberated on how to achieve a united and independent country.

In 1785, Franklin was elected governor of Pennsylvania, and he was one of the signers of the Declaration of Independence of the United States and the U.S. Constitution. During his life, he promoted the abolition of slavery and signed the Treaty of Paris, which ended the American Revolutionary War.

He was able to achieve all of this with the equivalent of a second-grade education. Benjamin Franklin's self-development was on account of his constant self-improvement, his perseverance, and striving to develop the right habits. For all the reasons that I admire Benjamin Franklin, his autobiography is one of the books that I recommend to those who wish to be successful and achieve their dreams.

I find inspiration in Franklin's method of facing personal and professional challenges head on. Thanks to his teachings, among other things, I quit smoking without too much difficulty. For the first three weeks, I kept a cigarette in my shirt pocket. When the desire to smoke set in, I would walk outside and breathe in fresh air for a minute. Then I would hold the cigarette and say to myself, "This piece of paper cannot dictate my behavior. It does not control me and I wish to have clean lungs." I kept breathing fresh air, and the desire to smoke would disappear.

At the pizza store, the interior was completely finished and we had spent more than two weeks testing the pizzas until they met my standards. One afternoon, a group of teenagers who had just finished a basketball game came into the pizzeria and asked if it was open. We said no, but after they had left, it occurred to me that they could help us by testing the pizzas that were about to leave the oven at that very moment. So I left the store and called out to them, "Do you want to try a free pizza?" The fatigued young men were obviously very hungry. They agreed and wolfed down a margherita pizza. I proposed that they return each day to try different pizzas, all free of charge, and to give us their feedback. For two weeks my "guinea pigs" came every day at 6 PM to give us their opinion on the pizzas that we had prepared.

Finally, on November 11, 1987, the first Pizza Phone opened its doors to the public. In an effort to convert all of the neighborhood residents into customers, we made a huge tactical mistake with the first offer. With the purchase of a slice of pizza, we gave another slice for free, creating a huge backlog of orders due to the different ingredients requested on each pizza slice, making the operation in the kitchen unmanageable. Customers would line up around the block. The initial discount offer lasted for two weeks. We realized that if we did not offer a discount of some sort, sales would fall dramatically. So we decided to launch a new offer, this time for a whole pizza, but only on weekdays, as weekends were already busy and did not require a discount.

I was still working at Johnson & Johnson when Pizza Phone first opened. I would leave the office at 5 PM and go directly to the pizzeria, where I worked until midnight. Pizza Phone was the first pizzeria in Spain with home delivery and it was a success. We would take orders until 11 at night.

Soon after opening we realized that we had more customers at the beginning of each month.

We prepared the dough for pizzas in the evenings and put it in sealed containers that were kept in a refrigerator so that it would ferment over 24 hours. Of course, we had some setbacks related to the temperature and the formula to make the dough. For example, one employee decided to put less yeast in the dough without realizing that it could seriously affect the flavor of the pizza.

When I tried a slice I knew that something was wrong, so I started to investigate what had happened. The culprit was reprimanded, but not fired and that mistake never happened again. In time he became a store manager. After that serious episode, I decided that we should have a central supply unit to control the formula. After all, our slogan would soon be "The Secret is in the Dough," so we had to deliver on that promise.

Unfortunately, almost every original partner of Pizza Phone failed to comply with the task that they had been assigned. They thought that because they were shareholders, they could act as they pleased. One of them even showed up with his wife one night at about 11 PM just to eat free leftover pizza. Fortunately, I was in the second-floor office and an employee informed me. From that day on we decided that employees and shareholders could buy slices or a whole pizza at half price. It was a matter of common sense, which, by the way, is the least common of all senses.

Unfortunately, when we began pizza home deliveries, there was a confrontation with one of the partners. Prior to this, we had come up with a guideline for when to deliver the pizza on foot and when to deliver it using our secondhand van that we had acquired. One day, when I gave an order to the deliveryman to deliver the pizza in the van, he told me that one of the partners had taken it to deliver another order to a house around the corner.

When the partner came back, I told him that the use of the van was unauthorized and that he had disrupted the workflow. He arrogantly retorted that he was a partner, just like me. At that moment, I realized that I was better off managing this business on my own.

My brother Eduardo arrived for a family visit in route to Rome with a stopover in Madrid on Thanksgiving Day, which was only two and half weeks after we had opened Pizza Phone. During his visit, I remember his constant criticism about everything, which I brushed off as typical of someone not in the business. It is easy to endlessly criticize when you arrive late to a project. I think the only thing he liked was the pizza. His stay in Madrid was a brief one, only two days, but after his visit, I started to send him monthly financial results, which we did by hand on a daily basis. He quickly realized that sales were growing astronomically every month.

We went over who our new customers were, who ordered home deliveries, the percentage of sales of the customer base, and the total sales, which were skyrocketing from month to month.

We had established work systems and strategies to measure our results, and it was easy to see that there was great potential to start a chain of home delivery pizzerias. I wanted the business to grow and my brother Eduardo wanted to join Pizza Phone as a shareholder and in the management of the company in order to participate in the growth of the business. I accepted Eduardo's proposal to participate based on certain conditions: (1) We would create a new company and I would own 60 percent of the business and he would own 40 percent; (2) I would always run the business as the CEO; and (3) Eduardo would be in charge of looking for business locations, supervising the development of the new-store construction and finding and screening potential franchisees.

We decided together to start negotiating with the original partners of Pizza Phone in order to buy them out. I was disappointed because of their unreliability and although only a year had passed since we opened the first store, we offered them far more money than they had invested. Ultimately we bought 60 percent of the company stock from the other partners of Pizza Phone.

I already owned 30 percent, and there were only two partners who stayed, with 5 percent each. It took us quite some time to close the negotiations. It coincided with the opening of the second store on Cochabamba Street, next to Paseo de La Habana, which eventually opened under the name of TelePizza.

To those who want to be entrepreneurs and have investors as shareholders, I advise you to own the majority of shares. The shareholders speak and vote at the shareholders meeting, according to the company statutes and the percentage of the business that they own. This is the meeting where the members of the Board of Directors are elected. The Board of Directors is in turn responsible for safeguarding the shareholders' investment. The board is responsible for recruiting and appointing the CEO of the company, who in turn runs the company through an Executive Committee.

To increase sales, we left coupons in neighborhood mailboxes highlighting our discounts for the week. We increased the delivery radius to two miles, which, of course, created other problems because we only had the old vehicle for the required longer deliveries. The driver of the van would drop deliverymen off at different sites and pick them up when they were done. On more than one occasion, the driver forgot to pick up one of the delivery guys, forcing that person to walk back to the store in the middle of winter. We came to realize that the most effective way to deliver orders by vehicle was to use mopeds. We bought several used ones, with great results initially. Soon, the old bikes began breaking down and we decided to replace the old mopeds with new ones. A breakdown did not just cost money to repair, it impacted our ability to increase sales!

Each day we ran sales report by street, building, and household, and once every six weeks placed coupons in mailboxes.

If the doorman of a building did not allow us to enter and leave the coupons, we had to be creative. On one occasion I showed up at a building saying that I was interested in buying the apartment after seeing a posted "for sale" sign. The porter very kindly showed me the flat, while four of my employees snuck in behind me and left coupons. It was a truly creative and intense year.

During this time I had continued working at Johnson & Johnson from exactly 9AM to 5PM. Soon there was gossip that one of the top executives was demeaning the role of being a Johnson & Johnson executive by working at night at a pizza store, dressed in blue jeans, a white polo shirt, and a red baseball cap.

Shortly before opening our second store, I spoke with the President of Johnson & Johnson, Spain, and told him that I wanted to leave as amicably as possible and was willing to negotiate whatever terms were appropriate. To my great surprise, his reaction was completely hostile and irrational. He ended up firing me, but not before paying a large severance package that I immediately invested into TelePizza.

I called the owner and President of Unilab Inc., Harold Bevelheimer, whose company produced Surgibone. In one and a half years the annual sales of this product had grown from 130 to 300 bones. Mr. Bevelheimer insisted that I continue to sell them. "Under no circumstances can you leave," he told me. "You are responsible for the increased sales, and I want you to continue being the distributor."

I insisted that I had left the medical-surgical sector, but Mr. Bevelheimer would not listen. I thought that if I accepted his offer, Johnson & Johnson would interpret it as an act of revenge on my part. In the end, I decided to open an independent company to distribute the bovine product and to hire a medical doctor, José Manuel Escribano, a salesman I knew from my time at Critikon, to promote the product throughout Spain.

I asked three more people to participate as shareholders in this enterprise, two of whom were the faithful Pizza Phone shareholders, and we became the distributor of the product for the next four years. We increased sales by 300 percent, reaching 900 bones per year. At the high point of the business, net profits (after tax) were increasing and were in the range of $250,000 per year. Unfortunately, coming around the corner was the big outbreak of mad cow disease, which affected the business enormously. Mr. Bevelheimer had to shut down his enterprise.

From my experience with Surgibone and mad cow disease I observed that one's eggs should not all be put in one single basket, because suddenly someone can pull the rug from under your feet and you will fall down.

This is good advice that I have not applied to myself in almost any of my ventures.

16

THE BEGINNINGS OF TELEPIZZA

We opened the first TelePizza store on Cochabamba Street one year to the day after opening our first and only Pizza Phone store. The new TelePizza store required an initial investment of 60,000 euros to buy out the prior tenant's rental contract, which was at a very favorable monthly price. New-market rental contracts were freely negotiated, yet under the rent control law, if an individual bought out an existing rental contract, it restricted the landlord to a maximum rental increase of 15 percent. Current rental prices in that area for properties of that size were around 2,700 euros. However, as we had bought out the existing contract, the landlord could only legally charge us 1,080 euros for the monthly rent. I viewed this payment as a partial purchase of the property. Actually, when the rental prices skyrocketed, our rental of the Cochabamba store became a real bargain.

The amount of rent a business pays can represent a significant percent of the total expenses of an enterprise. I view rent as a fixed cost.

But one of the most valuable lessons any business person should learn is that the biggest expense in any business is not increasing sales.

Most executives focus on controlling labor expenses or reducing the cost of goods sold by 1 or 2 percent. In my opinion, this can prevent sales growth, which is what significantly increases the market value of a business.

This time, we had one year's experience and well-trained personnel. We dedicated a full month to training new staff before opening the doors to the public. In the new store, we also added a walk-in cooler and two ovens, each with the capacity to cook 72 family-sized pizzas per hour. On weekends, during peak hours, we sold more than 140 pizzas per hour.

It was important to create the brand, and the word TelePizza was very easy to say. We added the prefix "tele" to the workers' clothing, as in telepolo, telecap, etc., and when the staff answered the telephone they would say, "Which TelePizza would you like?"

There was no doubt that the name was very catchy and becoming first in the mind of the customer. In fact, we even had difficulties registering the trademark, because we were told that it was a generic term. We were surprised, but we eventually got the trademark approved and it most certainly achieved distinctiveness and secondary meaning in the market. As a result, when asked today, I recommend registering a brand's trademark *before* launching a product.

There are companies like Procter & Gamble, for example, that have dozens of products, but none of them have Procter or Gamble in their names. This company has been around for more than 100 years. By contrast, Johnson & Johnson, which was also founded more than 100 years ago, has its name on almost everything it sells, from diapers to talcum powders, shampoos, dressings, and much more. So there is no fixed rule when it comes to company names and trademarks. With that said, I prefer that the brand, the company, and anything else one can imagine, are all under one umbrella. I have even been introduced at many meetings as "Mr. TelePizza," as if "Tele" were my first and "Pizza" were my last name.

A company must always aspire to be number one by size or by offering a better-quality product. If not, it should settle for no less than being number two. I am not the first person to have offered that advice and applied it to real life. In Jack Welch's book *Change or Someone Else Will*, he explains the theory clearly. He offers the example of soft drinks. It is the perfect, classic example. The Coca-Cola brand is on top, followed by Pepsi Cola at number two. A very distant third is Royal Crown Cola, or RC, as it is known in the marketplace.

The first TelePizza store had 1,100 square feet with two entrances. One entrance was for the public and the other for pizza delivery personnel. The location happened to be on the corner of the street, which was a huge advantage. The public could watch the pizza makers press and stretch the dough ball from scratch. Kids, our best customers, loved it best of all. Of course, it was also important that grownups could see through the glass window that the pizza was prepared fresh in a very clean environment.

Sales continued to rise to levels that I had not imagined possible. On a single day, we had sales of more than $8000.00, and I knew that we would continue to grow. I was unafraid of competitors and believed, even with only two stores opened, that we could franchise the whole country.

Franchises were something we gave serious thought too. We felt that Spain's top markets, such as Madrid and Barcelona, should be reserved for company-owned stores, with tertiary markets covered with franchises. We were approached by many potential franchisees who wished to open two, three, or more stores. Many of these inquiries were from experienced businessmen with the required capital to invest. Soon we were opening many stores, quickly.

We signed several types of arrangements. For example, we created a 50 percent partnership with two Americans, waving a royalty and franchise fee. We operated it and we shared the marketing expenses through a 3 percent fee to cover national advertising of the chain. They financed 100 percent of the investment of those two stores as part of the agreement.

The city of Santander hosted the first franchise outside of the Madrid province. My brother Eduardo, who was in charge of new-store development, including new franchises, was too hasty in signing the agreement. He did not take into account that the city is more than 400 kilometers from Madrid. This meant that the cost of shipping the ingredients and materials to the store, twice a week, would exceed the revenue that could be earned.

From this I learned that there are certain expenses that must be distributed among different profit centers and that trucks should never travel half empty. It was not a good situation, but it helped us to properly plan a good strategy for future store openings.

A number of financial groups requested meetings to discuss becoming shareholders of TelePizza. One of them even offered us a credit line of just over 2.4 million euros in exchange for 51 percent of the business. My brother and I had a discussion about it, but ultimately I decided to reject the offer, since I was not willing to give up the majority share or control of the company. Our lawyer then introduced us to a group of Spanish investors, not in the restaurant sector, to whom we sold 20 percent of the company for a capital injection of a little over $1,000,000. Thanks to this capital increase, in 1990, we were able to focus on opening company-owned stores.

The deal was a good one at the time and it contributed to the success of the venture, but it was one that would come to haunt me years later.

The performance of the stores was beginning to be well synchronized, running "just like a Swiss watch." Then, there was an incident at one of the stores. It was burglarized, which led me to take serious security measures. From this experience we decided to install two separate safes. In one of them, we kept only the cash that was needed to operate during the day, and only the store manager had the key and the combination. In the other one, the sales from the day were deposited whenever they exceeded 150 euros. The security company had the key to the second safe and collected its contents twice a week.

We also installed alarm and video surveillance systems. These measures helped us to reduce the petty theft from the cash register. However, our biggest problem was the theft of the mopeds that we used for delivering pizzas. After we had opened more than 100 stores in Madrid, we had as many as 500 mopeds stolen in a single year. The police realized the seriousness of the situation and began to help get the thefts of our mopeds under control.

I am of the opinion that the citizens of a democratic country must collaborate with law enforcement agencies and through cooperation we did see some improvement. On one occasion the city's police force asked us to help them detect pizza delivery orders that had been placed from specific cellular telephone numbers. The police were able to arrest some of Madrid's most dangerous criminals and we were grateful for the reduction in crime!

After we had opened six stores, we realized the importance of having a competent manager and three assistant managers to cover the two shifts per day, seven days a week. The management talent of the people responsible for the store stood out by the sales increases and by the behavior of the employees. So we decided that when a franchisee was about to open his or her first store, the manager would be sent to Madrid to be trained at one of our company-owned stores.

In 1989 we opened six new stores, growing to eight stores in a single year. The most famous of our pizzerias was on the corner of Juan Bravo and Prince of Vergara Street, in Madrid's Salamanca neighborhood. Being situated on the corner, it had great visibility and the area was full of bars that were popular among young people. Without a doubt, that store helped the TelePizza brand gain popularity.

Many celebrities came to be regular customers of the company. The Pilar neighborhood store was often visited by renowned athletes and thanks to the detailed records that we kept, I can confirm that the American professional basketball players living in Madrid were among our most loyal customers at both lunch and dinner time. When a pizza order was placed by any of the American players on the team, tips tended to be particularly generous, so the pizza deliverymen were always delighted to deliver those pizzas.

In 1989 we opened a central warehouse and dough production facility on Azucenas Street. It was just 1,000 square feet, and we used it only until the opening of store number 18 in 1990, when we had to find a larger place. We found a 6,000-square-foot site on the road to Andalusia between the cities of Pinto and Valdemoro. The Azucenas Street site became our centralized motorbike repair shop, which helped reduce the need for moped repairs enormously.

Obviously, the administrative part of the company was also growing. As I have previously stated, the first office was on the second floor of the Melchor Fernández Almagro store, in the Pilar neighborhood. The next one was installed in one of the rooms of my brother Eduardo's rented apartment, which was located two blocks from the Cochabamba store. Only two accountants worked there. When we got big enough, we opened another office in a rented apartment on Pío XII Street, which was 1,800 square feet, with a living room, kitchen, four bedrooms, and two bathrooms.

During the summer of 1990, we decided that in order to continue the growth of the company, we needed to interview college graduates so that they would one day become area supervisors and even future country managers as we grew internationally. We ran an ad in the newspaper to start the selection process.

The strategy was the same one that I had used at Johnson & Johnson. The text said, "Multinational company wishes to interview bilingual college graduates of both sexes who wish to make a career." And bingo! We received more than 600 résumés, and the store operations manager began reading them all, one by one. This task was consuming so many hours that the supervision of the stores was left unattended. I decided to look for someone from among the résumés we had received, whose profile was appropriate to lead a Human Resources Department and interview prospective candidates. Among those picked was Marilina Vílchez Jordán, who was born in the city of Linares, in the Jaén province. Marilina was a psychology graduate from the University of Granada with postgraduate coursework in Human Resources from Pontificia Comillas University (ICADE) in Madrid. I interviewed three other candidates for the position, but I chose Marilina. I chose well. The Human Resources department grew substantially, due to the significance it had to the company.

This particular hire was significant for another reason: Three years later, Marilina and I would fall in love. I had no idea then, but I was interviewing my future wife and the mother of three of my five children. My guardian angel was looking out for me again!

A four-ton refrigerated truck delivered supplies up to the north of the country where we had franchised stores in San Sebastian and Santander. At first, the truck was only loaded with dough balls in stackable drawers, which were sealed so that the dough would remain fresh. All the other required raw materials were purchased locally by the franchisees.

It did not take long before franchisees realized that the list price from our warehouse was substantially lower. Within a month, we were delivering all the raw materials required to run the stores from our central warehouse in Madrid. I told my brother that he should sell more franchises in the same geographical area, so that the refrigerated truck would travel fully loaded, delivering the dough balls and the raw materials to more stores on the same route. We sold franchises in Oviedo, Valladolid, Bilbao, and other cities during the next 12 months. The result was lower transportation costs for the delivery route to the north of Spain.

At the end of 1990 we had 18 stores, 17 in Spain and one in Lisbon, Portugal. The following year the number of stores continued to increase exponentially to 42. Now we had pizzerias in Spain, Portugal, Mexico, Poland, Colombia, and Chile.

In that same year the opportunity arose to buy 18 Pizza Hut franchised stores in Buenos Aires, Argentina. I traveled to the Argentine capital and offered to purchase the stores at an agreed upon price. Once I was back in Spain, I sent three executives to perform the corresponding due diligence of the franchisee's company. I also asked the leader of our group to write a draft of a contract of the verbal agreement that I had reached with the sellers. After a week, the contract was still not drafted, because one of the partners of the Argentine group was asking for an increase of more than 50 percent of the agreed upon price.

I told the three executives that if our counter-parties did not respect what was agreed upon, they should take the first plane available and return to Madrid in the next 24 hours. They did just that.

A week later, I received a phone call about renegotiating the deal. I told him that I do not do business with people who do not keep their word and that I was no longer interested. Twelve months later, I heard that they had to close all 18 stores. There is nothing worse than someone who thinks they are above everybody else. As the saying goes, those who always want more sometimes end up with nothing at all! Another variation is: *pigs get fat, and hogs get slaughtered.*

17

DIFFERENCES OF OPINION WITH MY BROTHER

After opening so many new TelePizza stores together, it became increasingly obvious that my brother and I had very different visions. In my view, he had poor knowledge of the operational part of the business and this caused misconceptions and conflict. Even through 1995 his part in TelePizza started and ended with finding suitable rental spaces, negotiating the rental contracts, overseeing the construction of new stores and seeking new franchisees.

My brother had a limited role in the company. He did not have the faintest idea about how to manage the warehouse where all raw materials were stored, let alone how to manage a store. The worst part was that he thought the business was as easy as blowing bubbles. He figured we should open new stores in more European countries. I disagreed because in order to do that, we needed skilled personnel, selected with extreme care, and we needed to train them in Spain to know how to implement the company strategies. This would require a huge investment of capital, which my brother was not taking into account.

Since we did not agree, and to avoid further confrontations, I suggested splitting the world into two halves. I would be in charge of Europe and Africa while he would be in charge of North and South America. At that time we had already opened stores in Mexico, Chile, and Colombia, and some of the partners in those countries were friends and old classmates of his from the Wharton School of Finance at the University of Pennsylvania.

Eduardo wanted to implement a dramatic growth strategy. This required almost unlimited funds to open more stores in the Americas. Although he had much more money than we had used to get started in Spain, he soon ran out of it trying to keep existing stores open, let alone expanding into new markets. It seems that the famous Wharton School of Finance did not teach him well, or he did not learn the importance and the implications of a cash-flow statement!

It took me some time, but in the end I learned one important lesson from all this turbulent experience with my brother: members of the same family should not work as executives or employees in the family business. It is better for the family that they remain on the Board of Directors of the company supervising professional managers. It is very difficult and unpleasant to have to criticize a relative, because it often results in a family rift.

As my brother and I quarreled, I decided not to allow relatives to work in the company. This was advice I did take, even to point of dismissing Marilina, my future wife, when we got engaged. We are still happily married, so in this case the advice worked out!

Since Eduardo had run out of money, he asked me for additional funds, to which I responded that I was concerned about investing in a financial bottomless pit. I asked him to present a business plan for his area of responsibility and if our shareholders accepted his proposal, I would not oppose it.

He never developed the plan. Instead, he opted to withdraw from the company's management team and demanded that I find a buyer for his 32 percent. The company bylaws did not provide a way out for shareholders who wished to sell their shares. Usually, investment and private equity funds will only invest in a company if the bylaws include a forced exit, either via an initial public offering or a trade sale.

None of the shareholders had taken this into account, and I did not open TelePizza with the idea of selling it. So, I started the search for a buyer of his shares.

18

THE GROWTH OF TELEPIZZA IN SPAIN

Sometimes we wish for the clock to stand still, but the passage of time never stops. As my father used to say, "The calendar is never-ending." From the time I decided to start my own business, it took me one year to open the first pizza store. However, it seems like it happened only yesterday. After a few years in exile it became clear to me that it would be at least a decade or more before I could return to Cuba. Once I realized this, I concentrated my efforts on becoming as productive as possible in my profession and eventually reached independence by owning and running my own company.

Many years ago my ancestors managed their own businesses, back when Cuba was a colony of Spain. After the 1898 Spanish American War, both of my grandfathers started and created very successful businesses as Cuba became an independent republic.

By 1992, we had signed franchise contracts in a number of cities, in Galicia, Asturias, León, Valladolid, Santander, the Basque Country, Valencia, Andalusia, and Extremadura. This covered the majority of Spain. Some were for multiple stores, but the majority of the agreements were for single pizzerias. It was easy to sell the franchises because we had a proven track record of success with every store that we had opened.

We kept working to cover new territories on the outskirts of Madrid, as well as in the capital city. Our main objective was to provide proper service to each and every customer, even as stores became overwhelmed with delivery orders during the peak hours. For stores stretched beyond capacity, we had to reduce the number of houses they served in their territory. This was accomplished by opening new stores to meet the growing demand.

As we opened new stores in strategically placed locations, we were able to continue growing and providing good customer service. The growth of the business prompted many requests for franchises. Store managers and some company executives wanted franchises and we always tried to accommodate them in the best possible way. We even created Cofrade, SA, a franchise holding company of which TelePizza, SA, controlled 51 percent. The remaining percentage was offered to a number of employees and executives, so that they would have the opportunity to continue in their jobs and, at the same time, invest and profit from the growth of the business. We had to be creative to attract the personnel necessary to continue growing, provide them with adequate training and ensure that we retained them.

We began transporting the dough balls and other products to the stores with our own refrigerated trucks. One night, a man who aimed to provide that service for us came into the shop. He had a stake in a transport business and had recently become a shareholder of a company that was granted TelePizza franchise contracts in Valencia and Valladolid. This new franchisee convinced my brother Eduardo that it was going to be more cost-effective to outsource transportation to a specialized company.

This issue caused further disagreements and arguments between my brother and me. He argued that the franchisee's transport company had a lower price for tires and gasoline, and therefore the transportation of raw materials would be less expensive. I did not want to add an extra link to the supply chain. I knew it would increase our costs, but my brother insisted and I did not want to create more animosity.

Since the business was very profitable, I accepted the proposal and decided to negotiate the contract. After jointly reviewing the document with the owner of the transportation company, he sent the final draft for my signature.

Thanks to the experience I had acquired with distribution agreements at Johnson & Johnson, I had developed the habit of checking every line, word, and comma of each sentence. This really allowed me to avoid problems. In this case, the smart cookie encountered a tough nut to crack. Upon reading the final draft of the transportation contract, I noticed that a new clause had appeared that had not been discussed, much less agreed upon.

He wanted to be paid a minimum amount for each trip regardless of the volume of products. Just as quickly as it had appeared, the clause disappeared. I deleted that clause from the contract and gave instructions to rewrite the contract under the terms already agreed to by both parties. I signed two copies and sent both of them for his signature. A few days later I received the contract back, signed by both parties. Several months later, at the end of the year, we received an invoice for an additional amount, so I ordered the invoice to be returned. This prompted the owner of the transportation company to visit me with the invoice in hand. I told him that that payment had no basis, and then he pulled out the contract. He was looking for the clause that he had included on his own and that I had deleted. He could not score the goal he wanted, but, in any event, he made plenty of money with TelePizza.

Meanwhile, TelePizza did not stop growing. The offices on Pío XII Street had become too small, so we decided to move to a larger facility that was almost 4,000 square feet, located on Guatemala Street, near Madrid's Plaza del Perú.

I clearly remember the business meetings in the office of the person in charge of direct marketing and advertising. When we exceeded 125 stores, we decided to launch our first national TV advertising campaign. We met with the marketing director and two franchisees that had prior consumer marketing experience. One of them suggested we interview different advertising agencies to see which one offered the most creative idea.

It was decided that one of the first things we needed was a slogan. We wanted a slogan that would be both representative of our product and difficult for our competitors to replicate. The phrase was then going to be repeated in each advertisement until it became first in the mind of the customer. I knew our product better than any other person present at that meeting, so all the questions were directed toward me.

I said that when we started the business, more than one customer commented that they loved the taste of our dough. Then someone stated that there must be a secret in the bread formula, and simultaneously another one said that the secret must be in the dough. It became immediately clear that "The Secret is in the Dough" would be our slogan. It was the best brainstorming session in which I have participated in my entire professional career!

An advertising fee of 3 percent of sales was included in our franchise contracts, but this was not invoiced until we had sufficient stores covering the Spanish market. We started collecting it from the franchisees, because the TV stations required payment in advance. It took several months to accumulate the necessary funds. The franchisees began to complain, some of them excessively, of this 3 percent charge that they were paying while not receiving any benefits of the advertising campaign. Obviously, they stopped complaining the day the TelePizza brand appeared on a TV commercial.

Bingo! Sales increased dramatically. The effect of the first advertisement was amazing. The phones started ringing seconds after the advertisements aired, and they did not stop. It was like magic. All of a sudden the franchisees felt they were part of a company that implemented plans and strategies that increased sales, substantially benefiting everyone.

Slowly but surely, the slogan was catching on in the minds of the customers. In 1992 we started with our advertising campaign. Simultaneously, that same year, during the World Exposition in Seville, our franchisee in that city, Manuel Prado y Colón de Carvajal, obtained the permits to open two stores and four kiosks at the fairgrounds on the Island of Cartuja. This further increased our brand's popularity. Seven years later, in 1999, the results of a survey reflected that 97 percent of respondents knew what our slogan was. There was no doubt that we had hit the jackpot.

We improved our direct marketing strategies substantially. Our system of door to door "couponing" became so perfect that Mr. Wilson Harrell devoted an entire chapter of his book *Total Quality Entrepreneurship* to explaining how we had been able to get everyone, even the deliverymen who worked part-time, involved in the objective of increasing company sales through couponing.

I met Wilson in 1993 at a pizza convention in Las Vegas, Nevada. Each year, more than 5,000 pizzeria owners meet to discuss, teach, and learn the best practices in the business. The convention offered different plans and strategies about the pizza business.

I remember going to Wilson Harrell's presentation, "How to Be an Entrepreneur." It was enormously enlightening for me. He said that, due to his behavior as an entrepreneur, many people had called him a madman during his lifetime. While he spoke, I immediately saw myself reflected in his words and ideas. When the lecture ended I turned to him and asked, "Do you do consulting outside of the United States of America?" He responded, "It depends where." When I told him it was Spain, he handed me his business card with a positive response.

Three months later, he visited us in Madrid as a consultant. We were two madmen, that is, two entrepreneurs, sharing ideas. I hired him because of his age (he was 74 years old) and because of the large number of businesses that he had opened and closed during his lifetime. I learned a lot from his successes and failures, and, above all, I learned that the idea to undertake and start a business is a normal one. Consequently, we were not crazy.

His book *Total Quality Entrepreneurship* explains that entrepreneurs go through four different stages during the lifetime of a business. The first, the genius stage, is when the idea for the product or service starts to develop. At its inception, the entrepreneur appeals to other people, and they all work many hours without pay or for insignificant wages, but are offered a stake in what they hope will be a large enterprise.

The second stage he labeled the "benevolent dictator." The company increases sales, and the entrepreneur, or founder of the company, makes all the decisions. He can have up to 20 people under his command, and the second stage is the one in which the entrepreneur thrives and is at his or her best. However, there comes a time of realizing that he or she has to delegate. In my case, I had 22 people reporting to me. Sometimes the day ended and I had not been able to devote adequate time to each one of my subordinates.

Necessity forces the entrepreneur to move on to the third stage, that of the "disinterested director." This is usually when the entrepreneur sells the business. During the third stage they are forced to delegate the decision-making to specialized managers and distance themselves from the main activity of the business. In other words, the founders become bored!

I think that I was at this stage when I hired Wilson Harrell. I thought he would help me make the transition successfully from the third to the fourth stage, which he called "the visionary." During this stage, the founder has properly delegated the company functions to a competent individual and focuses on personal matters, undertakes and supports philanthropic issues, and supervises the CEO through the Board of Directors of the company he founded.

In 1992 the CEO and six other executives from Pizza Hut visited us with the intention of exploring the possibility of buying out TelePizza. We had a very strange first meeting. They were dressed in navy blue or dark gray suits as if they were Brooks Brothers models, while I wore blue jeans, a white polo shirt, and Top-Sider shoes. The contrast was shocking. They wanted to buy 100 percent of TelePizza, and the price would be derived from a formula, which, according to them, was very advantageous to me, the seller.

They talked at length about how, in similar situations, others that had not agreed to sell had ended in ruin because of the opening of Pizza Hut stores nearby. It was the carrot and stick approach. If you sell us the business, here is the carrot, and if not, we will use the stick on you. It was an outright threat!

In any case, they asked me to think it over for a few days and said that they would return for the answer. They returned a week later and we met in the same conference room, with similar attire as before. They asked me if I had thought about their proposal and I told them I had. I proceeded to explain that I had applied the number of TelePizza stores to their formula and by my math, I would be paid $70 million.

They looked at me, puzzled, and said that was impossible. They tried to push for a lower number, but I interrupted them. "Wait," I said, "I do not want to sell even for $70 million. If you want to be first in the market, the price is $100 million."

Of course, they emphatically repeated that it was impossible. One executive termed it a "slap in the face".

It had a chilling effect on the meeting.

They repeated their old threats, stating they would flood the market with 150 stores and that I would live to regret my decision.

It did not take me long to reply. "Frankly, I would enjoy your coming to town," I said. "I'm a little bored and would welcome a world-class competitor."

After the 1992 investment boom caused by the Barcelona Olympics and the Expo 92 in Seville, there was a small decline in the gross domestic product of the Spanish economy. To my surprise, Pizza Hut followed through and created a wholly owned subsidiary that opened the 150 stores they'd promised. According to our management, sales began to flatten across the country as a result of this new competition.

I had heard every possible excuse, so I decided to prove to the TelePizza executives, supervisors and store managers that we could continue increasing sales if we kept applying the company's operational strategies.

I called a management meeting at the TelePizza headquarters with the top management. I started by asking for reasons why they believed there was no sales growth. There were many and theoretically convincing excuses. I asked my secretary to bring in Régulo Coronado and Perico Español, the only two store managers who were increasing sales in their respective stores and achieving objectives despite the supposed newly competitive environment. They told their success stories and the top management became embarrassed when they realized that all these two successful store managers had done to increase sales was to implement the strategies defined by the company.

I asked all the executives and managers present in the room, "Out of all of our stores in Madrid, which is the one that, in your opinion, cannot improve its sales performance?"

Everyone agreed that it was store on the Santa María de la Cabeza Street. They reasoned that the residents around that store were elderly people that did not eat pizza. On the spot I made the decision to work at that store every day of the week, from 10 AM until midnight. If my team wanted to see me or speak to me, they could find me there. I was determined to demonstrate that if the strategies were implemented, sales would increase.

A few months earlier, the marketing director and I had established the School of Magic program, just one of our many strategies used to increase sales. We traveled to Hong Kong, where we licensed 60 magic tricks at reasonable prices.

Upon our return, we hired a full-time magician to create five videos in which he showed how to perform the tricks to friends and family. It was especially geared toward children. With the purchase of two TelePizzas, those that belonged to the School of Magic received a free trick. After getting the 12 tricks of the first video, they could get the second one, and so on, up through the five videos. Our young customers, after eating 120 TelePizzas with the School of Magic and having fun with 60 tricks, not only remembered the brand but also the slogan "The Secret is in the Dough," and TelePizza became their product of choice.

A number of us reached the conclusion that we needed to add one more person to each store, so that every direct marketing strategy could be implemented. The newly created position would involve visiting nearby schools to offer the school principal an educational experience outside of the classroom, at the nearby TelePizza store.

The store supervisors were required to recruit the direct marketing specialist (DMS) for each store. However, the supervisors were reluctant to increase their staff numbers, claiming that it would result in an increase in stores' fixed costs. Like most managers, they thought that cost cutting contributes more to the bottom line when in reality sales increases add more profit and value to the company.

When I started working at the Santa María de la Cabeza store, I immediately realized one of the reasons why sales had not increased. The employee work schedules were poorly prepared and sales were being missed due to lack of personnel during peak hours.

The manager was not complying with all of his duties and the supervisor was not on top of this issue. Once I started working at the store, sales jumped more than 20 percent in the first two weeks just due to having a little extra staff, i.e. me, who had not been incorporated into the work schedules. Sometimes, on isolated occasions, managers and supervisors went out to deliver the pizzas and I stayed back at the store. One night we were so busy I summoned the supervisor and the regional manager responsible for the Madrid stores. I would not authorize the phones to be taken off the hook, which was the usual practice when the schedules were poorly prepared or the store was understaffed. When these managers arrived at the store, there were more than 20 pending orders to be delivered in their corresponding thermal bags. They started taking the pizza orders to their destinations, surprised at the extra volume.

Sales began to rise at other stores as well, since no one wanted to be surpassed by the store in which I was working full time. All in all, I spent four months in the Santa María de la Cabeza store, which was long enough to shake up the organization and develop and implement the DMS position. The role of the DMS included a number of functions.

The first role was to visit elementary schools in the area of distribution of TelePizza stores, to get all children between the ages of 6 to 11 years of age to visit the store one day a year during off-hours between 11 AM and 1 PM to enjoy a fun activity and learning experience. In Spain, regular lunch runs from 1:30 to 3:30, so this did not interfere with our busy lunchtime. This program worked to perfection in the Santa María de la Cabeza store, which was the first one at which this was implemented.

The second DMS function was reviewing the work schedule. Thirdly, they were in charge of interviewing potential employees, so there was always a pool of candidates to hire whenever necessary. Fourth, no employee could answer the phone until they had received proper training and the approval of the DMS, who ensured that all standard operating procedures were being applied.

The fifth function was supervision of the couponing by the deliverymen and the pizza makers working part time.

The DMS positions were mostly held by female university graduates. It was a full-time job, demanded a lot of time, and its goals were easy to measure. When visiting the schools there was some reluctance from the schoolteachers at first, but it did not take long before they were the ones who called us to coordinate the pizzeria visits.

Between 20 and 30 children attended each session, and we spent two hours with them, explaining everything from the ingredients in the dough (without revealing "the secret" of course!) to the origins of the pizza itself. We made it a fun experience for all involved. We explained that the original pizza was just bread, tomato, and cheese and that years back it was called pizza Margherita in honor of a princess from the cheese-making region of Parma. She had graced Naples with an official visit, and forever after was associated with cheese pizza!

We taught them the importance of hygiene during the preparation of the product, and when they were hungry, they would create their own TelePizza, in groups of five, with the ingredients of their choice. Everything was free. We would give them, as a gift, the first School of Magic video and the first trick. Also, we gave them as a gift a "telecap" with our logo and a picture that we took of them in front of the store under the sign, wearing their telecaps.

We assured the students that the picture and the pizza making diploma of TelePizza would be sent by mail to their homes. In return, all we asked was that each student fill out a form with his or her address, telephone number, and date of birth.

Finally, a sixth function was the birthday program – inviting the children back to celebrate their birthday at our stores. We were extremely family friendly. Children could celebrate their birthdays in the store with their friends. At their birthday party they would go into the kitchen and, as pizza makers with a certificate, were qualified to prepare their favorite TelePizza. The DMS would call the children's mother one month before the date of their birthday to coordinate the party, which would take place from 4:30 to 6:30 PM, provided that it would not affect the operation of the store during peak hours. It was a big hit.

After those four months in the Santa María de la Cabeza store, I came to the conclusion that the position of DMS was essential. It not only helped increase sales but enabled us to be first in these students' minds because of the fun activities.

Shortly after that, we opened another store in that same neighborhood that our managers had universally agreed lacked sales potential. Both stores worked like a Swiss watch, which is how I like to see things operate. It had become clear to me that there can be a gap between the person who invents or develops a new strategy and those responsible for the implementation of it.

As an owner, when your company is successful, you must ensure that company executives do not become "drunk on account of their own success". It is easy to become too relaxed and no longer maintain the proper discipline to comply rigorously with the strategies that led to success in the first place. Nothing motivates better than the President of a company competing against the management team at each one of the stores to increase sales. Nobody wants to be outdone, especially by the boss!

Most of the Pizza Hut stores that opened in the following two years were within 100 yards of our pizza stores. They thought they would make us go bankrupt. However, as I always say: "God helps those that help themselves." The opposite occurred.

Between 1994 and 1995, out of the 150 stores that Pizza Hut had opened, they had to close 30 of them and the company in Spain became a graveyard for CEOs. None of them met their sales and profit targets. In a business like this, you always have to be above the break-even point. If you are below it, losses can be in the millions of dollars.

One lesson learned, probably by both TelePizza and Pizza Hut, is that when sales are stagnant, the highest authority of the company must get involved, getting into the guts of the business. The CEO is the one that must identify which tasks and processes are not being implemented properly. He should know the difference between a real reason and mere excuses provided by the directors of the company.

For instance, we had a serious problem in the Logroño store, which was part of the Basque Country franchise. Although sales in Vitoria and Pamplona were climbing, at Logroño, they could not exceed 18,000 euros per month, while others surpassed 60,000 euros. The franchise owners blamed the idiosyncrasies of the city's inhabitants, without analyzing the store management.

The franchisee informed me that they wanted to close it. I did not immediately accept. Instead, I offered to keep the store and buy all the equipment at the same price that they had paid when the equipment was brand new.

They accepted immediately and I went there with one of the best store managers of Madrid, Perico Español. We performed an audit and agreed to formulate an action plan. We quickly realized that the store conveyed the feeling that it could close at any time. I wanted a radical makeover. We bought 20 mopeds and put them in front of the store, so we were giving the neighborhood the impression that we delivered TelePizzas in large quantities. We also put out attractive offers to increase sales at the same we were staffing up to a level more appropriate for a store selling 32,000 euros a month. We began putting coupons showing our discounts in all the mailboxes in the entire area. Sales doubled in less than three months and after one year we had to open a second establishment in Logroño. Three years later we had four stores there.

It seems appropriate to point out here what an interesting thing it is to observe the behavior of some human beings. Often their ego does not allow them to accept a simple piece of advice. The person who ran the Logroño franchise had succeeded in the other TelePizza stores that he had opened. He was successful in running the stores, so he came to the conclusion that the culprit behind his only failure was the culinary culture of the citizens of the city. According to him, practically all the inhabitants of Logroño had a plot of land from which they fed themselves, and did not eat pizzas. Our customers being from Logroño, how were they going to drink a beverage other than wine!? A brilliant excuse! It served its purpose and the franchise owners accepted it.

Meanwhile, on a personnel level, Marilina led the Human Resources department at that time. One Saturday I asked her to accompany me to a photo shoot session, so that I could have her opinion. She accepted with enthusiasm, and after seeing the photos, I invited her to see the movie *Havana* at a theater nearby.

Afterwards we went to dinner, during which I told her that we would get married and would have many children. She always says that it was not a question, but rather a statement.

When you want to sell an idea, sometimes it is best to state an outcome as a fact. Going directly to the point is an important and effective communications strategy.

Even so, it took us a while to get married. I was still technically a Cuban citizen and the wedding was delayed because of the excessive time it took to acquire the documents required by the Spanish government from Cuba, including my birth certificate. I picked up the wedding ring at the jewelry store an hour before the ceremony. It was worth the wait. The wedding, which took place on June 9, 1992, was attended by many people related to the company, franchisees, shareholders, suppliers and, of course, members of our respective families.

In 1993, our first son, Alberto, was born, and from the first moment his eyes were wide open. He watched everything around him, showing great curiosity. It is a feature that he has maintained over time and in my opinion is without a doubt a guarantee of success.

In December 1994, Andrés was born. He had to stay for quite some time in the neonatology section of the 12th of October Hospital in Madrid. He was born with a metabolic deficiency, and several consultations with different doctors revealed that the only solution was a liver transplant. We weighed the possibility of having it done in the United States, but we opted for the 12th of October Hospital, because Dr. Enrique Moreno González, who had extensive experience in this type of surgical procedure, was a member of the staff. The operation took place on the last day of August 1996. The tragedy and the generosity of a family gave Andrés a new life. He is now 19 years old and still a fighter.

Between 1991 and 1995, our lives were moving at full speed. On a professional level, we were engaged in the competition with Pizza Hut, and at the same time, we had to fix what my brother Eduardo had left unresolved in Mexico, Colombia, and Chile after leaving the company. On a personal level, the delicate situation of Andrés was the top priority.

TelePizza kept moving and growing at a good pace. We employed a team of three people full time to seek future store locations. We hired Carlos Gray as head of the store development department, to control the implementation of the new pizzerias. Several surveyors were responsible for the supervision and everything worked very well. I can say that this area of the company was never a cause for concern. They were all highly motivated to have all the new stores opening on time and within the budget.

At this time, we also put together the information technology department. Before 1992, I had tried to develop, with the help of different technicians, the software needed to properly manage the business, but we did not get the results we wanted. At the beginning the cost of the department seemed high, but over the years, I became convinced that the investment we made was worth it. By the time I sold my shares in the company, in 1999, the computer system allowed me to monitor and analyze sales in detail and on a daily basis, highlighting what was right or wrong in each store in the chain worldwide.

The accounting department also worked properly and did so from the beginning. The three people who started it came from Johnson & Johnson and had more than 10 years of experience. I absolutely trusted them.

Since my brother Eduardo had asked me to help him sell his TelePizza shares, I prepared a business plan and met various investment banks that would be interested in buying the block of shares that Eduardo wanted to sell. The best offer was based upon a 60 million euro valuation for the entire company.

We signed a confidentiality agreement, and the investment bank began their due diligence, the customary analysis of the company. They were almost finished when I had a very heated discussion with the head of the group that was performing the audit. A dispute occurred that ended when the banker insulted me. I asked him and his entire team to leave the premises, because I did not want to do business with someone so disrespectful and arrogant.

This upset my brother because he was very close to cashing in and becoming a very wealthy man. I explained that there were two issues. First, the investor imposed conditions that did not exist in the bylaws of TelePizza SA. Secondly, and more importantly, I did not want to do be saddled doing business into the future with an investor and business partner who had disrespected me.

My brother complained to other shareholders and told them that I was not allowing him to sell his shares. In so doing, he managed to find other shareholders of the company who were also short of cash and needed to sell their shares. Suddenly, the initial capital increase for twenty percent of the company reducing my 50.1% share of the business to 40% loomed larger than I ever could have imagined and cast a shadow over my life.

19

FIRED FROM MY OWN COMPANY

In September 1995, I convened an ordinary shareholders meeting to inform everyone about issues relevant to the company. I thought it was going to be like any normal shareholders meeting. Little did I know that I was walking into a firing line. My brother Eduardo with his 32 percent ownership of the business, was teaming up with other shareholders with a plan to remove me from the Presidency. It was their aim to take money out of the business and sell their shares in the company. Together, they held over 50% of the shares. I called the meeting to order and before I could move into the agenda a lawyer representing these minority shareholders interrupted, calling a motion removing me as President. It passed, and I was fired.

I was down, but as the single largest shareholder, I was not totally out. The board had a fiduciary duty to ensure the business was run properly and there was no corporate waste. I was determined to return to the company I had started and I still owned a significant piece of it!

Obviously, this was a devastating turn of events. I started the business. I had accepted my brother's request to join TelePizza and it was always very clear to Eduardo that I would run the business. What my brother had orchestrated was unthinkable to me.

The shareholders now wanted me to sell my shares, so in addition to firing me, they also tried to make my personal life difficult. Our one-year-old son Andrés was very sick and waiting for a liver donor. At the time, our family was living in a house rented by the company. Shortly after I was fired, the new Human Resources director that Marilina had hired to take over her position came by the house to deliver an eviction notice removing me, pregnant Marilina, Alberto and our sick son Andres out of our home. It was a totally unnecessary and spiteful act by my own brother and his allies.

Ironically, their plan to make me sell might have worked if they had not been blinded by their own greed. My entire net worth was invested in TelePizza and I was penniless. This was actually a joke I used to tell my friends who inquired about my net worth to which I would respond "all I own are pizza ovens and mopeds". A couple months in this predicament and I would have been forced to sell.

Fortunately, my guardian angel was looking out for me again. In their lust to loot the company's cash reserved to finance growth of the business, they could not simply write themselves checks – they had to issue a dividend. This is exactly what they did, perhaps forgetting that I owned 40% of the business. To my great delight I opened my mailbox to find a check that shored up my financial position. As I have said before, *pigs get fat and hogs get slaughtered.*

Shortly after this time we celebrated Marilina's birthday with an expected surprise, the birth of our youngest son Alfonso, on February 22nd, 1996. Some people believe it is good luck for a mother to share a birthday with her child. We call it good family planning!

While I was gone, the operational department heads in charge of all store operations in the country met and drafted a document supporting me. It was signed by 47 of the 50 executives present. The document stated that they disagreed with the decision to remove me from the presidency and offered me unconditional support. It was given to Javier Gisbert, director of operations.

He forwarded it on to the Executive Vice President of the company, who had been my second in command. When I found out about this document, I requested a meeting of the operations department personnel to take place in front of the TelePizza executive offices.

I called the Executive Vice President. He objected to going against the new Board of Directors, and from the tone of his voice, I knew that he had tried to call off the meeting. My intuition told me immediately that he was part of the conspiracy that had stabbed me in the back. It is worth noting that his part in this was a shocking and unbelievable betrayal. I had recruited him to join TelePizza and incentivized his performance with 5% of the business, which had made him rich. Those shares came from me personally, and were not newly issued shares from the company. My brother had refused to allow dilution of his shares, so they had all come from me!

He was not the only one. The number three man of the company talked to a number of top executives to let them know that this issue would be resolved one way or another. He suggested that the time had come for me to leave the company and predicted that I would sell my shares for the well-being of everyone. Based on all these half-truths, veiled threats and rumors, the top executives of the operations department started meeting with the supervisors and convinced almost all of them not to support me.

Only a small group of five people stood up to management. Régulo Coronado, Juan Bautista Galán, Jerónimo Moraleda, Iñaqui Mella and Perico Español were store managers and supervisors. To this day I call them "The Magnificent Five," because after meeting with their superiors, they came to inform me about the shenanigans being pulled by top management. They were totally opposed to the unethical behavior they were witnessing. Perico Español was particularly vocal and ended up being fired for standing up to them.

When the new President and his entourage took over TelePizza, sales were growing at a rate of 40 percent per year when compared with the same month of the previous year. After just nine months under the new leadership, sales growth dropped month after month to just 7 percent. The shareholders, who represented 60 percent of the company, thought that they could easily sell their shares in the company, but that did not turn out to be the case.

These shareholders could not take the company public at the valuation they wanted because the sales growth had evaporated. To make matters worse for them no banks or individual investors wanted to buy my shares in TelePizza unless I would sign a non-compete agreement, which I was not about to do. It is worth noting that if I had been bought out as they wanted, I would have been capitalized with perhaps 30 million euros. I would have immediately turned around and started opening competing pizzerias. Suddenly, they found themselves in a Catch-22.

Even the Santander TelePizza franchisee's father-in-law came from Miami to Spain, along with his brother-in-law, who was my uncle José Pujals, to try to smooth out the situation between my brother and me. They did not succeed in their endeavor and only told me that greed had taken hold of my brother.

The "Magnificent Five" and I began to plan the opening of a new pizzeria under a different brand. Out of the blue, my brother called me one day, probably because he was aware that the monthly growth of TelePizza had fallen four-fifths since I had left the presidency of the company. He asked me to seek a solution that would satisfy both of us.

The new pizzeria was never opened and we decided that I would look for a financial group to buy my brother's shares. The first one that showed an interest was Cofir, an investment group led by Gabriele Burgio. The majority shareholder was Carlo de Benedetti, owner and founder of the Olivetti Company, which was in serious financial trouble at that time. From what I understand, the Cofir advisors recommended that they invest in TelePizza SA. However, when the Italian press found out about the potential deal they published a front-page article criticizing Mr. de Benedetti for investing in a pizza business in Spain. An Italian newspaper even published a front-page photograph of him wearing a chef's hat. Cofir's financial investment came to nothing overnight.

At the same time, my lawyer got me an interview with some of the directors of BBVA, one of the most important banks in Spain. In order for this bank to become an investor, we were required to take the company public within six months of the bank making its investment.

For the shareholders who no longer wanted to be part of the company, a public offering would give them an exit. About 20 percent of the shareholders thought that going public would not be a success, so an agreement was reached with them whereby the bank would buy their shares immediately. Simultaneously, Eduardo, who now wanted to sell his shares in the initial public offering (IPO), signed another agreement with the same bank, which required him to sell all of his shares in the IPO. An additional condition attached to BBVA's investment was that I would return to be President. However, they conditioned this return upon my agreement that I would not fire any TelePizza executives until we were quoted on the Madrid Stock Exchange. It was a bitter pill to swallow, but I agreed.

It was an unfortunate turn of events that we had lost time in our battle with Pizza Hut. Had the 1995 coup d'etat not forced me out, I am convinced that we would have forced Pizza Hut to withdraw from the market and the IPO would have been that much bigger. Who knows how many millions of dollars my brother and the other minority shareholders lost, first through their greed and then by selling too early.

20

TelePizza Goes Public

Back at the helm of TelePizza, I had to concentrate on injecting adrenaline back into the executives of the company in order to return TelePizza to 40 percent annual growth. As this new phase of the business unfolded, I was going through a whirlwind of different experiences in my personal life. For instance, two months after I had returned to TelePizza, Andrés received his lifesaving liver transplant.

When "the Magnificent Five" and I got back on board running the company, there was one executive who did the honorable thing and resigned from the company without asking for severance pay. His name was Jorge Galofré. He was an area manager and he had fired Perico Español for speaking up on my behalf. His resignation was in keeping with his promise that he would resign if Perico came back to the company.

On account of Galofré's departure, the two remaining area managers had to divide the country in half. At the same time, I positioned two trusted managers as auditors to verify that the strategies were implemented correctly in each store.

The two area managers accepted the new management scheme. However, one of them wanted a raise, stating that he was now managing more territory, half of the country instead of one-third of it. I told him that I would consider it and would let him know the following day.

The following morning I met with the two area managers and the two auditors and proposed a new way to manage the stores. There would be four executives, instead of two, covering all of Spain. Even though the four executives would have less territorial responsibility, I told them I would not reduce anyone's salary. Thus began a co-management system, not just in store operations but in a number of divisions of the company. This was to address daily administrative issues that arise and, simultaneously, continue with the proper supervision to ensure the implementation of the strategies in the stores.

I did not perfect this co-management system, but I am sure that it was the right way to properly structure the company at that time. The four executives, two for each half of the country, competed against one another. This served as a catalyst to increase productivity and sales before taking TelePizza public. I personally supervised the area managers and caused the spark required to increase sales at a faster rate. From June 1996 to our November initial public offering (IPO) just five months later, we increased the sales growth 40 percent, compared to the same month a year earlier (before my dismissal).

We also implemented the new co-management system at the supervisor level. One person supervised 15 stores a month with a checklist, and his or her co-supervisor was involved with only a single store, the one with the worst performance at the time. Their goal was to fix it no matter how long it took, from within and from the top down.

Each month the two supervisors switched duties so they would be equally involved in various tasks. Both the co-management and co-supervision structures caused a formidable competitiveness among the teams and motivated them, which allowed us to implement strategies to near perfection.

We focused first on implementing the couponing strategy, because we had to get back to delivering the appropriate number of coupons to each and every household. We also focused on improving the training of our telephone operators. Thanks to this endeavor, the average customer order total increased by approximately $1.50. Also, the launching of the triple-decker pizza and a barrage of television commercials helped us grow.

During the autumn of 1996, before the IPO, I had numerous interviews with different media. Due to this national media attention, consumers had a more positive perception of our brand, which greatly helped our credibility as a company for the future. My brother Eduardo negotiated the IPO with the banks. Everyone selling shares were paying the banker fees proportionally to the number of shares sold. The company did not need money to grow and was not issuing new shares. BBVA was responsible for the sale of shares in the domestic market and Merrill Lynch led international sales.

The gist of the deal that the bank negotiated with all parties was one to resolve a family dispute. The bank demanded that my brother allow me to come back, and required me to come back to run the business. Then, I had to sign a personal guarantee pledging my shares as collateral to the bank that I would not fire any executives before taking the company public. I also committed that the IPO would occur within a six month period. If the company did not go public within six months, I would literally forfeit my shares to the bank. For his part, my brother had to sign a personal guarantee, secured by all his shares, pledging to sell all his shares in the IPO. If he reneged, he would forfeit his shares to the bank.

In the weeks leading up to the IPO, greed began to once again take possession of my brother as he realized that selling his shares *in the IPO*, rather than *after*, was not advantageous. He was the one who had negotiated the IPO price with the bank at a company valuation of 130 million euros. Later on, Eduardo realized that the bank had priced in a "25% pop" to provide an incentive for IPO buyers, which by definition meant he was leaving money on the table. Now he wanted to sell *after* the IPO, so that he could enjoy the 25% pop! He threatened to back out and the bank had to call Eduardo's lawyer to remind him that he had signed a contract in which he would forfeit his shares if he did not follow through.

The IPO date was set within the six-month parameter required by the bank. Ten days prior to the IPO we began what is known in the trade as the "roadshow", i.e., presentations to institutional investors, in November 1996. We presented our business plan to investors over five full days to investment funds in Madrid, Barcelona, Paris, London, Copenhagen and Zurich, and then back again to London.

The presentations were a hit. We covered the institutional investor allocation quota after the very first meeting and the banks' advisors suggested that I downplay expectations in the rest of the presentations. My years of experience selling ideas and products at Kirby, Procter & Gamble, Johnson & Johnson and TelePizza were shining through.

Of course, it helped a lot that the company's sales growth had risen to 40 percent over the previous year. The bank recommended being conservative and only forecasting 25 percent growth per year over the next three years. During the roadshow, I explained the strategies of couponing and the school visits. Just when they thought there were no more strategies forthcoming, I spoke about the School of Magic and the video gifts with tricks that came with an order of two TelePizzas. They were laughing wholeheartedly when we explained that, after 60 tricks and 120 pizzas, we called the children's mothers so they would invite their kids' friends to celebrate their birthdays at the store. In short, investors were convinced that TelePizza would continue growing and increasing its market share.

At the time of the IPO, we had more than 50 percent of the pizza market sold in stores. When investors asked me what I feared most, I always said that the only competition that worried me was our own incompetence, because it was easy for our young managers to "become drunk with their own success" and forget to implement the strategies that we relied on for our success.

At the end of the roadshow, the shares were oversubscribed 64 times. On the first day of trading, the stock closed at 18 euros, 30 percent above the offer price. The company's value now exceeded 200 million dollars, and under these conditions, we were invited to the Madrid Stock Exchange trading floor. I asked the head of TelePizza store operations in Madrid to instruct the direct marketing specialists to be available to hand out TelePizza slices to all the traders and investors present on the trading floor. Without a doubt, we livened up the trading floor and our success spread across the Madrid stock market.

For the first time in a long time, I felt satisfied. After a long wait full of complications, the effort had been worthwhile and the overwhelming success of the IPO compensated for all the disappointments of the previous year.

We went to celebrate our accomplishment with some friends over lunch at the Zalacaín restaurant. That night I thought about all the previous TelePizza shareholders who had been bought out by BBVA and about how they had behaved in the past. In the words of an old proverb, "Wait in the doorway of your house for the cadaver of your enemy to go by." It is also said that "He who laughs last, laughs best."

My commitment not to dismiss anyone until TelePizza was listed on the Madrid Stock Exchange had now expired. Initially I fired only two people. Dismissing employees can be a very unpleasant task, but this time I did not have any remorse. Those two people were expecting it and there was no doubt in my mind they deserved it.

The TelePizza phenomenon, as many called it, was in full swing. The store growth in all countries where we had invested grew from month to month at a very high rate. This was not the case at other pizza chains. For example, Pizza World could not compete with us and the owners came to us offering to sell their business. We decided to go ahead with this acquisition, but we ran into an obstacle when not all of its franchisees were willing to change their store name to ours. We were very close to breaking off the negotiations.

At first, we offered them 12 million euros for the 120 shops, but the name issue prevented us from closing the sale. Then I opted to offer about half a million fewer euros for the acceptance of either names. I thought we could somehow manage. Plus, I added a Spanish Pure Breed colt for Arthur Carulla, a member of the family that owned Pizza World. The seller's executives met for half an hour and, upon their return, signed the agreement and we were able to finalize the purchase. Mr. Carulla, who behaved like a gentleman during the negotiations, never picked up his colt, which became a stallion and is already 17 years old.

An IPO in general is a very unique learning experience that is not taught in business schools. Actually, you can only learn about the stock exchanges if you work for an investment bank, or if you personally have listed one or more companies on the stock market, whether it be the Madrid Stock Exchange, the Dow Jones, or the NASDAQ.

In my opinion, there are several reasons to list the shares of a company on the capital markets, such as when the company is overindebted, needs more money to continue growing, or when banks, before lending, want to see a better ratio of the company debt relative to the EBITDA (earnings before interest, taxes, depreciation and amortization). This debt-to-EBITDA ratio should be between 2 to 1 and 3 to 1 or, at most, 4 to 1. Another reason for listing a company is to get the best possible price when some of the shareholders want to sell some or all of their shares. I have seen the benefits of both situations. At TelePizza, the underlying reason for going public was to get the best possible price for the shareholders. In the case of Jazztel, years later, we first sold convertible bonds, and later, shares, to increase the liquidity of the company and facilitate its growth.

The main disadvantage for the management of any company in going public is the need to certify and report financial results on a quarterly basis and respond to questions from analysts, investment fund managers, and minority shareholders. Another disadvantage is the lack of privacy in regard to the main shareholders' equity, since everyone knows the number of shares owned by those who control the business. Multiply the number of shares by the listed share price and it is publicly known what your theoretical net worth is. The public's perception of the main shareholder changes radically. In my case, I was no longer Leopoldo Fernández Pujals. I came to always be referred to as "the guy from TelePizza" or more humorously, "Mr. TelePizza".

Another negative factor is the effect on employees. Many expect their salaries to increase in proportion to the value of the company. If stock options are offered to executives, this shifts attention to the share price and away from the business. It is what I call "becoming drunk with success."

In any case, to go public, or to get your company's shares listed on the stock market, the company's Board of Directors must receive the majority of shareholders' approval. The next step is to hire a law firm with specific expertise in this area and, simultaneously, you must select an investment bank that will execute the sale at the retail level and with the institutional investors, both domestically and internationally. The legal fees are relatively reasonable compared to the investment banks' fees. In Spain, legal documentation is prepared by the law firm and presented to the Comisión Nacional del Mercado de Valores (CNMV) for approval. Afterward the company and the investment banks define the percentage split between the retail and the institutional investors.

In general, it is optimal to have an adequate percentage at the retail level. In my opinion, a good split is 30 percent retail, 30 percent institutional investors, and if at all possible, the main shareholder should keep at least 40 percent. In this way the owner, despite not having 50 percent of the company, can maintain control. Also, to minimize the investment banks' fees, I suggest inviting several banks to bid for the IPO, as they will then compete and lower their commissions. Although it costs a little more, I recommend that the bank guarantee the sale of the shares.

After TelePizza's successful listing on the stock exchange, I became very much in demand as a speaker at universities. I cannot remember the exact number of entities that asked me to give lectures from 1996 until the end of 1999, but it was close to 100, and not only universities but also business associations in all of the provinces and regions of Spain. I remember I started to limit my public speaking events the day I realized that my secretary had booked a lecture every day of that week. It seemed like I was dedicating myself to satisfying other people's requests.

I remember I took a trip to Fort Lauderdale to visit my father and Kay. I told them that I wanted to buy a place for them on the beach. My father told me, "Older people are like old trees: if you transplant them, they will die." So he continued living in the first house our family bought after going into exile, and he stayed there until the end of his days.

In the creation of a large company, any entrepreneur goes through several stages. Logically, you must be aware that different areas of the business require more attention than others during various periods.

From my point of view, the time had come to take a step forward in TelePizza and to become a large multinational company. For this to happen, the first thing that needed to be done was to change the structure of the Human Resources department. It is my opinion the résumé and profile of the Director of the Human Resources Department should be different and have experience in the core part of the business. So we chose a director with proven experience in positions of leadership, supervision, and sales management of the stores. The next step was to restructure the training department, which had been created from the beginning to train both those who ran the stores and company executives. Previously, we had chosen outsiders with Human Resources or psychology backgrounds. Now, we handpicked the best store managers and supervisors to lead the training courses which were to be a prerequisite to grow in the career path at TelePizza. In this way, no one doubted that the company was giving them adequate training.

At the same time, we needed to develop and improve the training courses in order to have a sufficient number of executives who could fulfill their functions in their areas of responsibility. It was essential that every executive of the company was exposed to the proper managerial culture in order to achieve the success we all desired.

We made additional changes in the Human Resources department. We included skill tests in selling ideas and looked for candidates who were multilingual, with higher education. We created an evaluation and development department. Through the use of various evaluation tools, we made sure that the promotion and dismissal of employees would be as objective as possible. One of the policies of the company was that no one would be shown favoritism. Every candidate would go through the selection process and the corresponding evaluations. From these reviews we established the training plans that were tailored for all those employees who wanted to grow and develop within TelePizza.

Through the Instituto de Estudios Superiores de la Empresa (IESE) in Barcelona, we were contacted by a professor from the Harvard Business School. He requested a number of interviews with various executives in order to develop the TelePizza business case. We scheduled meetings that began at 9 AM and ended at 9 PM. He was astounded and could not believe that we worked 12-hour days. They were also surprised at how we measured everything that we did with such eagerness to improve.

My management philosophy has always been, if it improves the business, do it. If you do it, measure it to see if you are improving. The example I use for employees to understand the importance of measuring is that of keeping score in a sport. If no one knows who is winning, because no one is writing down the score, then no one would go to watch the game. In a company, all employees must work to achieve their individual objectives and measure their level of achievement. Each worker has to have the mindset of continual improvement. If not, they do not know if they are effective and cannot be compared to other employees. Measurements, updated data, and statistics give life to any enterprise. Let us not forget that human beings are competitive by nature and always want to be the best.

Even after selling my TelePizza SA shares in 1999, I continued to return to the Harvard Business School in Boston, Massachusetts once a year for the next five years. In the students' evaluation reports, I was rated as one of the best speakers, so the professor that taught the TelePizza business case kept inviting me back. I was flattered and this made me feel appreciated. Quite a few students, after listening to my lectures, kept in contact with me. In fact, a decade later I continue to get inquiries from some of them.

I felt comfortable with the growth and direction of the company. I had delegated my CEO responsibilities to two executives working jointly in the co-management system. I concentrated my efforts upon building a diverse Board of Directors that could provide constructive suggestions to the Executive Committee. Among the board members was José Ortiz, a lawyer who had served as secretary of TelePizza's Board of Directors. Three entrepreneurs whom I had known in recent years were also included. These were Angel Lozano, founder and owner of Redur, a transportation company that at that time had more than 100 trucks; Joaquín Cayuela, whom I met when our respective enterprises were chosen among the fastest-growing companies to participate in the Europe 500; and Antonio Catalán, whom I met when I was in negotiations with the Cofir company before the IPO. Antonio founded and directed the NH Hotels chain and, afterward, the AC Hotels.

Another board member who accompanied us during this first stage after the IPO was Alfonso Martínez de Irujo, who at that time was one of the administrators of the Instituto de Empresa de Madrid. The BBVA bank, despite selling half of its shares in the IPO, at more than double the price it had bought them, had two directors on our board, Julio Azcargorta and Juan Manuel Ruiz. Our Board of Directors was comprised of only eight professionals.

The growth in the number of stores and the increase in revenues and profits were spectacular. Quarter after quarter we exceeded analysts' expectations. The board meetings primarily served to relay to the board members how the company was progressing. Ángel Lozano often said that instead of being compensated for participating on the Board of Directors, he should paid for everything he learned as he listened to the strategies and management philosophies that allowed us to continue to grow at a high rate.

During this stage I went back to playing golf, a hobby that I had briefly picked up two decades prior, before going to Vietnam. TelePizza bought some membership shares of the Club de Golf La Moraleja, so executives who wished to play golf could enjoy the sport. In 1998 I met Javier de Toledo, CEO of OKI SA in Spain

At Doug Danser's wedding in Natchez, Mississippi. Doug is a friend, a fraternity brother and was my roommate during one of my semesters at Stetson University. Doug is in the center with two other brothers, Mike Egan and Robert Kimble.

Photo of the Executive Committee of Johnson & Johnson Central America & Panama at the home of the Managing Director, Mr. Dewitt Paul (Top Center). Three of us were Cuban Americans. I am standing in the Top Left Corner, Nicole is sitting on the armrest wearing black.

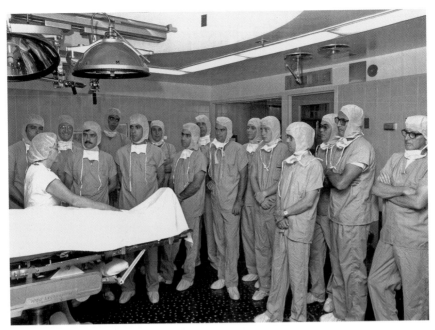

Photo taken at the Houston Methodist Debakey Heart And Vascular Center where Johnson & Johnson executives from Latin America gathered to view an open-heart surgery by Dr. Debakey. The explanation of the surgery was carried out by the head operating room nurse. I am front row, 3rd from the left.

Harold Bevelheimer and his wife, owner of Surgibone, Incorporated the maker of Bovine Bones.

With my oldest son Alejandro and my second son Carlos at the first Pizza Phone store in 1987.

Pizza Phone's first coupon flyer. Today it seems like a relic from the last century.

At our first TelePizza franchise store, located in Santander (Northern Spain). Mary Lizama (far left) and her husband Javier Echavarri, the store manager (wearing jeans) is pictured along with my wife Marilina and myself (center). Marta Lizama and her husband Angel Acha are to our right.

My father and his wife at the World Expo 1992 in Seville, Spain.

At the 1994 TelePizza Christmas Party giving Luisa Rodriguez her Tele-Polo and Tele-Gorro (baseball cap) commemorating five years of service.

With four of the Magnificent Five that backed me during the coup that ousted me from TelePizza. Left to Right: Iñaqui Mella, Jerónimo Moraleda, Régulo Coronado, myself, and Perico Español.

Sharing a smile with Juanba Galan, the fifth member of the "Magnificent 5".

This photo was taken at our farm in Segovia, Spain. In the background is the 13th century monastery San Pedro de las Dueñas. Pictured is my son Carlos holding the reigns of PRE champion horse Rondeño IX, alongside my wife Marilina and me. My youngest sons, from left to right, Alberto, Andres and Alfonso are standing in front of us along with Tele, our German Shepherd.

and Portugal. We agreed during this encounter that the following year we would organize a golf tour so that Spanish professional golfers could have the opportunity to compete in a tournament twice every month and be prepared to compete abroad. It was named the OKI-TelePizza tour. The first tournament, in Valencia, was won by Miguel Angel Jimenez, a native of Malaga, who at that time was not well known, but who rose to prominence on the European Tour, the PGA tour in America, the Ryder Cup, and, recently, the Champions Tour in the United States.

Thanks to the golf tournaments, I had the honor and privilege to meet and play with the late Severiano Ballesteros and his brothers in the beautiful environment of the Pedreña golf course in Santander. I also had the pleasure of playing golf with Santiago Luna and his brothers, as well as with Sergio García, when he was still an up-and-coming amateur. I also played with his father, Víctor García, a great professional player and golf instructor. During this time I met Miguel Angel Martin, who introduced me to Carlos Suneson, the son of a Swede and an English lady, who married and remained in Spain living in the Grand Canary Islands. Carlos was born in Las Palmas, and at that time was the European golfer who drove the ball farther than anybody else, usually exceeding 300 yards.

Unfortunately, when I sold my shares of TelePizza, SA in November 1999, I disassociated myself from golf in Spain, and the new owners of TelePizza decided not to continue organizing the tour that we had started. I have fond memories of the final tournament of the 1999 OKI-TelePizza tour, which was held at the Monte en Medio golf course in Andalusia. I invited 10 Cuban-American friends from Miami and their spouses as well as some Cubans friends who resided in Spain, to participate in the Pro-Am. They were all delighted to be able to see firsthand some of the best professional golfers at that time. The day after the final, we organized a match-play competition at the Valderrama golf course, between the Cubans from Miami and those living in Spain. Those representing Spain won, albeit by a small margin. Later, when I was at Jazztel, we helped and supported both Gonzalo Fernández-Castaño and Carlos Suneson in their professional careers during the 2005 and 2006 seasons.

In the middle of 1999, businessmen Pedro Ballvé and Aldo Olcese asked me for a meeting to explore the possibility of TelePizza buying their fast food company, Telechef. I did a superficial audit and told them I was not interested. Despite this they urged me to analyze their company in greater depth, and so I asked them to give me a report of the customer orders, sorted by type of customer (new ones and repeats). It took them a few days to produce the report, and when they showed it to me, I told them once again that I was not interested.

There was not a doubt in my mind that Telechef's business was going bankrupt despite any amount of help anybody could provide. I explained to them that their sales were not growing because the percentage of repeat customers was minimal. The bulk of their sales was produced by advertising, which attracted new consumers just one time. Shortly afterward, Pedro Ballvé called me again, and I agreed to meet with him once more. He again asked me to buy his company, and then I said something that left him scratching his head: "Have you thought of buying my participation in TelePizza?"

He seemed baffled that I would consider it. He asked, "Would you be able to part with the controlling interest of the company that you have created?"

I responded, modifying that old Spanish saw that "More was lost in Cuba", adding "because of the Castro brothers".

The truth is that never in my wildest dreams would I have thought of selling the company, but that possibility was gaining momentum as I realized that the next step for the growing company was in the international arena. Going international meant many things, including the potential of me having to spend a lot of time traveling and away from my family. I had three small children, one of them with a transplanted liver. I could not and did not want to leave Marilina alone.

Moreover, for the previous three years, I had been involved in the tumultuous situation in Cuba. I wanted to help in whatever way I could to bring about freedom and democracy in my country. This dream required my involvement and constant work both in Spain and abroad, which was something that I could not have done if I continued working at TelePizza 100 percent of the time.

For these reasons, I decided to sell my first business, my dream of a lifetime. This dream had been accomplished over 12 intense and exciting years. In November 1999, I sold my stake in TelePizza to the Ballvé brothers and a group of investment bankers.

To summarize, I think that TelePizza achieved the following milestones:

1. The success of the IPO, which had a demand of 64 times over the number of shares that were offered to the market. That is, if we issued a number of shares worth 130 million euros, there was a theoretical demand for $7.5 billion euros of requests from investors, whether institutional or private. The banks had to reduce the allocation of the shares. If a buyer wanted 64 shares, he or she was only given one. Merrill Lynch and BBVA both commented that this had never happened before in Spain.

2. At that time stock option plans were very popular, but only for executives and board members, not for all full-time company employees. We were the first to create, and present to the CNMV, an innovative stock option plan for all full-time employees. I have always been of the opinion that if the company was doing well, shareholders should benefit, but employees, officers, and directors need to profit as well.

3. TelePizza began trading on the Madrid Stock Exchange on November 13, 1996, at a value of 130 million euros, and ended the day at 169 million euros. In less than two years, in May 1998, it reached a value of 1.8 billion euros. Until then, there was no other company in Spain that had appreciated so much, so quickly.

4. At a shareholders meeting, we approved a stock split. We divided by 20 the face value of each share. The nominal value was 100 pesetas, and we lowered it to 5 pesetas. My attorney asked: "How can we have shares for such a low value?" I replied with another question: "Is it legal?" It was, so we did, and it was a success.

5. We experienced very strong growth of the company, especially during my last three years, 1996 through 1999. During this time period we purchased the Pizza World chain with 120 stores. This was our main competitor, and after this acquisition we reached total revenue of more than 290 million euros, or 64 percent of the pizza restaurant market in Spain. In comparison, in the United States, Pizza Hut and Domino's controlled 22 percent and 16 percent of the pizza restaurant market, respectively.

6. In 1996 the Europe 500 organization selected the 500 companies with the highest growth rate during the period of 1991 to 1996. TelePizza appeared first on the list.

7. During my last year at the helm of the company, total sales surpassed that of McDonald's in Spain. To my knowledge, no other fast food company in any country in the world has achieved this.

8. TelePizza got to be listed on the Madrid Stock Exchange and it was included in the selective IBEX 35 index. To belong to this small group it is necessary to have both average trading volume and company capitalization value within the top 35 traded companies of the Madrid Stock Exchange.

9. It was an honor for us to have the prestigious Harvard Business School take an interest in us, and creating a TelePizza business case study to be taught to the students at that university.

21

THE JAZZTEL CHALLENGE: COMPETING AGAINST GIANTS

After the sale of TelePizza, I was already residing in the Bahamas and I truly got to step away from my professional career and focus on my family and some special projects that were very important to me. My wife and I devoted our time to the education of our three younger sons and helped my son Carlos open his first restaurant in the United States.

I also dedicated my time to the cause of freedom in Cuba. This included supporting the working group of former political prisoners, Plantados Hasta la Libertad y la Democracia en Cuba (Planted Until There is Liberty and Democracy in Cuba). Additionally, we provided financial assistance to the Fundación Elena Mederos, Human Rights First. Marilina and I joined forces to develop a special project closest to our hearts, Awakening Smiles.

During that time we also collaborated with the Alpha-1 Foundation, an organization based in Miami and devoted to finding a cure for the enzyme deficiency with which our second son was born. At the prep school where my father had been a Spanish professor, Suffield Academy, we financially and personally supported several initiatives. We donated the necessary funds to construct a classroom building in his honor that bears his last name, Centurion Hall. In coordination with the Academy, we created the self-development and leadership initiative, and implemented an alumni program to encourage children and grandchildren of alumni to attend the Academy. As previously mentioned, the effect of this motivated alumni to support the school financially and altruistically after graduation as well.

During the summer of 2004, I was on vacation in Mallorca, Spain, before travelling to the Olympics in Athens. I had just finished playing a round of golf with some friends when I met with some executives from Jazztel, a failing telecommunications company. They had come from Madrid to ask me to invest in their enterprise. We agreed to meet again when I returned from Athens, and then in September, I would ask my advisors to analyze their proposal in Madrid.

After three meetings in which Jazztel executives presented the financial situation of their company, we agreed to perform a thorough investigation and audit of the company. Essentially, this was a due diligence for a possible investment. Three of my trusted advisors, José Ortiz, Miguel Ángel Rodríguez, and Ramón Quintero, spent two weeks on the task. Two weeks later, before they finished, I had private meetings with each member of the Executive Committee. To my astonishment, these meetings were interrupted one morning because Jazztel's share value began rising precipitously to the point that it had jumped up 10% by mid-day (from 0.25 to 0.275 per share) with skyrocketing trading volume. I asked the company management to ask the CNMV to suspend trading of the Jazztel stock. It was suspended for a day and a half, which was all the time I would have to make the decision of whether to invest or not. Years later, I found out that one of the people who attended those initial meetings was fined close to 1 million euros by the CNMV for insider trading. The person responsible for those leaks was not one of my closest advisors.

After a four year hiatus from running businesses after TelePizza, I was looking forward to becoming involved in a new venture. In addition to feeling unproductive, I was looking forward a new business management challenge. I had heard many times that TelePizza's success was just luck, and that was motivation for me to prove to the naysayers that I could be lucky twice. Jazztel was in a sector, telecommunications, that neither my trusted team nor I knew anything about. We did know, however, that the company urgently needed a 15 million euro capital injection before the end of the year to save it from filing for bankruptcy. It was listed on the stock exchange and, in total, would need hundreds of millions of euros invested. Nevertheless, the challenge of competing with the telecom giants was very tempting. I realized the huge market potential that existed, and I assessed the investment already made in their fiber optics network infrastructure, which gave the company an advantage.

Many have said that it was a daring decision, but I trusted my managerial skills and my business experience and acumen. My guardian angel, once again, was on my side. When I informed my trusted group about the decision, they were floored. Before looking at Jazztel, I had given them instructions to find companies in which to invest. These enterprises should have been outside the technology sector with a good track record and growth potential, should have been profitable and have had less than 100 employees. Jazztel had only one of these characteristics (growth potential). As I have said, I do not have a good track record of following my own advice, but I am attracted to difficult challenges.

In mid-October 2004, I joined the Board of Directors of Jazztel, Plc. as President after investing nearly 90 million euros into the company as a capital increase. That investment made me the largest shareholder of the company, holding 24.9% of the stock. At the time of my investment trading had been stopped and the shares were valued at about 0.27 euros per share. As soon as it became public knowledge that I was going to be involved in the company, the value of the shares went up close to 50 percent.

At a press conference, I informed the media that in one month, I would present a three-year business plan. To implement this plan in a short period of time we changed the Executive Committee makeup almost completely. Also, many changes took place at the Board of Directors level.

The total debt of Jazztel was made up of a convertible bond of 110 million euros, which was incurring 10 percent annual interest. However, there was a clause that stated that if the share price were maintained above 0.66 euros for three consecutive months, the debt would be converted into shares. Fortunately, the market had reacted positively to my business plan, so we were able to convert this debt into shares.

We still had to find the funding required to implement the business plan. We met with several banks, but none of them would give us a loan or believed that a possible capital increase would be viable. However, they all agreed that we could issue new convertible bonds, which is exactly what we did in April 2005.

Interestingly, there was a world-famous investment bank that made every effort to make us fail, and that is when I realized that I was getting into a sector where I was considered an intruder. Even though one of our main competitors seemed to be using its influence to put obstacles in our path, the market liked our business plan and management changes. At the beginning, we had thought about a bond issue of 225 million euros, but we received over 1 billion euros of offers so we increased the convertible bond offering to 275 million euros.

During the first 90 days, two unique, noteworthy events occurred. The first one happened when one of the most important Jazztel executives, who had been part of the previous management team asked for a kickback of 100,000 euros from the company for bringing me into Jazztel. Such behavior was unethical, and since I was aware of other irregularities from this executive, I recommended an immediate dismissal for misconduct. This was acted upon and the executive was dismissed.

I firmly believe that company personnel should behave like the directors do and, in my opinion, "bad apples" should be discarded.

The next case left me perplexed. The secretary of the Board of Directors, José Ortiz, jointly with the CEO, dismissed 10 executives in a 72-hour period. The CEO, who seemed completely overwhelmed, told José Ortiz, "I do not know how you can sleep peacefully at night firing so many people."

When I heard this comment, I thought, "How can a top executive's hands tremble when he dismisses incompetent employees?" Yet another perfect example of the Peter Principle.

Offering a superior product was a top priority because my focus has always been on increasing sales. With that in mind, we invested in new ADSL 2 technology that would provide 20 megabytes per second, a speed that no telecommunications company offered before then. We connected 537 central offices with fiber optics that reached more than 60 percent of the households in Spain. That, coupled with a substantial investment in advertising, led to a great demand.

Simultaneously, we took the necessary steps to develop a CRM (customer relationship management) system to handle the thousands of calls from customers who wanted to sign up for service with Jazztel. However, something unexpected happened. Telefónica caused us a lot of problems in the portability of the telephone lines, and in most cases the delays were unbearable for the customers. On account of this, many customers canceled their orders with us.

We also encountered obstacles and delays in our fiber optics connection to the central offices. We attributed this to our competitor, too. Therefore, we initiated a series of actions and lawsuits. We filed 50 complaints, through administrative channels, with the Commission of the Telecommunications Market (CMT). Thirty-seven of them were resolved, all in favor of Jazztel. Unfortunately, the fines were paid directly to the Spanish government and not to our company.

Since Jazztel did not directly receive compensation for Telefónica's misbehavior, and the fines themselves were not enough to change their behavior, our advisors recommended going through the judicial channel and filing a series of lawsuits not only against Telefónica but directly against its Board of Directors as well. These lawsuits were based on the findings of wrongdoing in the those 37 CMT decisions. In the United States these actions would resemble anti-trust lawsuits.

We were taking an unprecedented action. The Telefonica Board of Directors were some the most powerful people in Spain. Many people cautioned me that such a thing just was not done against people of such prominence, notwithstanding that the allegations had already been substantiated!

During this time we had to reduce company expenses to survive and as the ramifications of the litigation settled in for all the parties, we began negotiations with Telefónica.

We assigned this difficult task to José Ortiz, our lawyer and secretary of the Jazztel Board of Directors. In the end, in March 2007, we reached a satisfactory agreement for both parties. Since then, Telefónica and Jazztel have had excellent business relations, and today the two companies are partners in the deployment of Jazztel fiber optics project.

Another area of which I am proud is with respect to Jazztel's customer relationship management (CRM) system. Almost every executive will hear at some point or another that the business cannot grow because their company's CRM is either poorly designed or does not exist. This was something I was hearing and so we decided to hire a top firm to build a CRM system from scratch that would meet all the technical aspects required to implement our business plan. The results, quite frankly, were astonishing and helped our sales grow. This was a case of understanding the difference between an excuse and a legitimate barrier to growth.

Regarding our customer service, I made a decision contrary to the trend in the marketplace, which at the time was in favor of outsourcing the call centers as a best practice. I remembered reading in a Peter Drucker book about Thomas E. Vail, the President of the first telecommunications company in the world, American Telephone and Telegraph (AT&T). AT&T's mission was one single word: Service. This core value helps to explain why that enterprise was never nationalized. It was this example that prompted me to keep our call centers in house, rather than entrusting them to outsiders. Outsourcing would have prevented us from rewarding the good telephone operators and from firing the bad ones. Figuratively speaking, I chose to go to war with our own soldiers. In the autumn of 2005, we created our own customer service center in Cordoba, Argentina, with more than 1,000 telephone operators. I do not have any doubt that sometimes in life it is better to copy what works, but on other occasions, it is better to innovate.

The following spring, in 2006, a London-based investment fund contacted us because they were interested in investing in Jazztel. The negotiations did not come to fruition, because we did not agree on the valuation of the company, but at those meetings, one person stood out. It was the man leading the evaluation who had an extensive background in technology.

One of my principles was that the heads of our Executive Committee for technology should have no ties to Telefónica, to eliminate any potential outside influences. Fortunately, this very polished executive seemed to have no connection to a Spanish education much less to Telefónica. So, during a stopover in London on my way to the Bahamas, I met with the Managing Director of the investment fund and asked him two questions. First, would he recommend this young man to be the CEO of Jazztel? If so, did he have any objection to me offering him employment?

After that meeting I proposed to our Board of Directors that we offer the post of General Manager to José Miguel García, who joined Jazztel on May 3, 2006. After six months he was appointed CEO of the company.

One of the most discussed strategic decisions of the Board of Directors was whether to acquire a virtual cellular operator license from Orange, so that we could offer mobile broadband to our customers. In February of 2008 we signed an agreement and launched Jazztel mobile services. This agreement remains in force today.

This was one of only two decisions that the Board of Directors did not approve unanimously, by one vote. Nearly seven years later Jazztel has approximately 1.685 million mobile customers. Although it may seem like any other strategy that was hit or miss, the fact is that if we had not made that decision when the market began to converge with the bundling of land lines with mobile, Jazztel would be in a precarious situation today.

We were going full steam ahead, but a black cloud was looming. In April 2010 our bond offering of 275 million euros had to be paid, and we did not foresee having the liquidity to make the payment.

One year prior to the due date, we started tough negotiations with the major bondholders that concluded with an agreement that was very advantageous to the company. It included a debt reduction of 70 million euros, with another 70 million euros coming in the form of a capital increase. We issued a new bond of 111 million euros, maturing in April 2013. This agreement went into effect in July 2009. We had previously purchased the remaining 24 million euros of bonds in the market, at a discount close to 70 percent, in the months prior to the agreement.

As the proverb says: "It is never too late if the outcome is good." Before the storm began unleashing its fury, we decided to be proactive and find a solution to the problem. I remember that in order to conclude the negotiations, I had to explain to the bondholders, by phone and at the top of my voice, that since we were in the same boat we needed to row in the same direction, or all of us would go down. I know from experience that, in negotiations of this kind, if you do not transmit strength and you are not ready to die killing, you will be crushed as if you were a cockroach.

As the readers may have noticed, Human Resources have always been an essential ingredient in my business success. One of my priorities going back to our ads seeking bilingual men and women college graduates was to find, hire and train talented female executives. With this in mind we adopted Proper Governance Practices requiring that at least two women serve on the Board of Directors of the company. We hired a headhunter that specialized in finding well-qualified women with experience either in telecommunications systems, marketing, or finance. Instead of two, we ended up hiring four very qualified women to be appointed to the Board of Directors to fill four recently vacated positions.

I wanted to bring about a successful managerial culture at Jazztel, just as I had done at TelePizza. So we began to give motivational speeches to all employees of the company, in which we explained our vision for Jazztel for the next five years. At the time that I invested in the company, Jazztel had only 5,000 ADSL customers. That's it! The entire value of the company was in the fiber optics that had been deployed and the customer growth potential. I made it our mission to reach 10 percent market share within three years. The audience in front of me listened in disbelief. I was obviously putting into practice the title of this book, we were shooting for the stars!

In September 2011, we reached 1 million ADSL customers. As of early 2015, the company had in excess of 1.5 million customers. Jazztel had achieved more than 12 percent of the market. Today, Jazztel's management is striving to reach the 2 million mark, and the company track record plays in their favor. They are shooting for the stars and they have already reached the moon!

As José Martí said, "Honor, honors." That is why I must congratulate José Miguel García, CEO; Vicente Casciaro, who had previously moved from Argentina to Panama to work with José Miguel and then came with him to Jazztel to be in charge of the network and systems department; and Ramón Quintero, director of the finance department, who previously worked in our family office. The three of them have played a very important role, along with the entire Jazztel team, achieving extraordinary results in a very competitive market after reaching an agreement with Telefónica in the spring of 2007 that allowed us to construct a successful business.

For Jazztel's immediate future success, it was vital to have a fiber optics network that could reach more than 50 percent of Spanish homes. We got down to work, and in October 2012, we were the first ones to reach an agreement with Telefónica to jointly deploy fiber. This allows Jazztel to reach 3 million homes. In 2011 it was not possible, but by the end of 2014 Jazztel finished the network rollout and is now working on increasing its potential reach to 7 million homes by 2017.

In April 2013 the company paid the last installment of its bonds, which allowed it to expand its debt capability and take on further investments in the fiber optics deployment.

That same month I had the honor and pleasure of seeing Jazztel enter the IBEX 35, the main stock market index of the Madrid Stock Exchange, developed by Bolsas y Mercados Españoles (BME), which comprises the top 35 companies by liquidity and market capitalization. With this accomplishment, I have been told that I am the only businessman in Spain who has placed two companies on that list. The first time we did it starting from scratch, and the second by taking the reigns of a company that was virtually bankrupt and had only 5,000 ADSL customers.

Professor Jay Lorsch from the Harvard Business School was interested in understanding how a small telecommunications company, near bankruptcy, could be injected with entrepreneurial spirit stemming from the Chairman of the Board of Directors. Professor Lorsch has spent decades understanding how boards of directors should be managed. We coordinated a three-day visit to Madrid by one of his assistants.

During this trip his assistant interviewed every member of the Board of Directors and the Executive Committee members that were there before 2007. After 90 days we received the proposed draft of the business case study. We approved it, and the Jazztel business case is currently being taught at the Harvard Business School. When I attended one of Professor Lorsch's classes, I was informed that they do not believe that any other entrepreneur has two of his companies being used as case studies at Harvard. It's an honor to be in rarified air!

In September 2004, Jazztel's market value on the stock exchange was approximately 150 million euros. Ten years after that "daring" decision, we have received a takeover bid for a value close to 3.5 billion euros, about 23 times more. Somehow, while we were competing with the giants, we became one of them. I guess I got lucky again!

22

MY DREAM OF A FREE CUBA

In 1996, José María Aznar was elected prime minister of Spain. I thought, naïvely, that perhaps Spain's policy toward Cuba would change. My uncle José Pujals Mederos, my mother's younger brother, was a political prisoner, a *plantado*, in several of Castro's prisons, for 27 years and 22 days. A *plantado* is a political prisoner who, morally, ethically, and patriotically does not accept the dictatorial regime and remains a rebel against the oppressors as long as necessary in order not to give in or give up on his or her unwavering principles. He was imprisoned when he was 36 years old and was released at the age of 63.

All *plantados* boast that they feel like free men behind bars. They refused to wear the common prisoner's uniform, so many of them remained in windowless solitary-confinement cells, naked and unable to see the light of day for years. They were unable to even communicate with other prisoners. In defining the prisoner's treatment, my uncle José said, "It was a colossal effort to destroy the dignity of men." It is clear that if the Castro regime had forced the *plantados* to dress like common prisoners, the words that Fidel Castro has repeated for decades, "In Cuba there are no political prisoners," might have seemed credible.

After selling my TelePizza shares, I stated during a press conference that I was going to support two organizations that were fighting for freedom and human rights in Cuba. In Madrid, the Elena Mederos Foundation: Human Rights First and, in Miami, Plantados hasta la Libertad y la Democracia en Cuba. The Elena Mederos Foundation was created with two main goals. The first one was to get

137

Spaniards to sponsor the families of political prisoners to help them survive while the heads of households were behind bars. Through the foundation, we sponsored about 300 families, giving them $50 a month. We funded the second goal, called Awakening Smiles, a project led by my wife, Marilina, whose purpose was to help Cuban children in need of urgent surgical operations that could not be performed on the island. I remember Wendy, a 5-year-old deaf-mute girl, who received a cochlear implant. Through an agreement with the San Rafael hospital in Madrid, we were able to help three children with different medical conditions.

The refusal of the Castro regime to grant more Cuban children permission to travel outside the country ended the project. I was told that the Castro regime was concerned that its image would be tarnished, since it had been portraying the island as a place where advanced medical treatment was readily available.

Miguel Ángel Rodríguez, a senior executive at TelePizza and a man in whom I trusted, led the foundation in Madrid from 1999 until 2004. When we got involved in Jazztel, he came to work at the company, along with three colleagues from the foundation.

Then the Elena Mederos Foundation moved its operations to Miami, where it was managed by those former political prisoners involved in Plantados hasta la Libertad y la Democracia en Cuba. The *plantados'* purpose, initially, was to travel around the world to democratic countries and give firsthand testimony about their experiences as political prisoners. They wished to create a response similar to that created by Nelson Mandela in South Africa. It is clear that the struggle against apartheid has received much more media support and attention than the fight for freedom in Cuba. As a result they changed their strategy and became involved in assisting dissidents who oppose the regime on the island, providing support to their families while they were in prison. The organization sponsored another 300 families, and after becoming responsible for the Mederos Foundation, they began to carry out their activities from within the island.

I supported the Plantados organization because I thought that anyone who joined the fight for freedom in Cuba would be considered, in fact, another plantado. The six men who created the group had served more than 150 years combined in prison. Five of them were in exile, and one, Julio Ruiz Pitaluga, whose time in prison stretched 26 years, had decided to remain in Cuba. He chose to stay on the island because he wanted to see the dead body of Fidel Castro prior to his own death. It was a desire that would not be fulfilled.

While Cubans suffer from the communist tyranny of the Castro brothers, too many foreigners, many of them Spaniards, are taking advantage of the cheap, almost slave labor that the Castro regime offers. I call this a modern system of slavery. For a foreigner to start a business in Cuba, he or she has to come to terms with the dictators who control the country. In this agreement, the Castro regime keeps the majority of the business and provides the land, stolen from its former owners, many of whom were descendants of Spanish citizens. The investor of the company can only hire Cubans authorized and provided by the regime. This further strengthens the regime as they dole out favored jobs to partisans and saddle opponents with back breaking work. The investor pays the government, the Castro regime, which acts as a "partner," $400 to $500 a month for each employee and from that money the worker only receives between $10 and $20 a month. Regime partisans end up in jobs that can accept foreigners' tips. The mainstream media does not report on this reality. The labor unions in democratic countries do not denounce this practice, even when the companies are Spanish, and successive governments continue to turn a blind eye.

The Cuban workers cannot go on strike, because the dictatorship created the labor unions in Cuba and they respond to the orders of the regime. The regime also controls the information provided about Cuba to the outside world and expels any journalist who intends to write or talk about the reality of the island. So, the Spanish citizens only know what the Castro regime allows them to know, and this is done with the approval, implicitly at least, of a large number of European and North American mainstream media outlets. That is why so many tourists still go to Cuba, misinformed and ignorant about what really happens on the island. Thanks to these foreign visitors, the regime continues to receive income from tourism, which is used to torment and oppress the Cuban people. This has been going on for more than five decades. I feel outraged when I listen to some newly returned tourists say that the Cubans are happy, always joyful, and that they do not stop singing. The tourist does not know that Cubans sing because they cannot speak out freely.

On more than one occasion I have been asked in Spain if now is a good time to invest in the island, before the Americans arrive. I always answer that we must not forget that Castro stole the land from its rightful owners and that sooner or later they shall recover it. I have also heard from Spaniards that Cuba "belonged" to Spain before 1898 and it is not correct for the Americans to gain control of the island. However, let us remind ourselves that since 1902 the island belonged to the Cubans, and thus to neither the Spaniards nor the Americans. In fact, according to the history books written by the Cubans, a war called the Cuban Independence War took place between 1895 and 1898. According to the Spanish historians, it was called the Cuban War, and according to the Americans it was called the Spanish-American War. In any case, Cuba remained a free, independent, and sovereign republic in the hands of Cubans. Since the citizens of each country during the last century have read the history written by their own historians, it is difficult to agree on what actually happened.

Among the five *plantados* in exile was Mario Chanes de Armas, probably the political prisoner who spent the longest time in completely inhumane conditions. In 1953, Mario participated, along with Fidel and Raúl Castro, in the attack on the Moncada barracks in the eastern region of Cuba. It was 16 months after Fulgencio Batista's coup d'état on March 10, 1952, which established a dictatorship on the island. After being captured, Mario Chanes de Armas was tried and served time, along with Fidel Castro, until 1955, when he was released from prison by an amnesty law. Mario followed Fidel to Mexico and accompanied him on the *Granma*, the ship that brought the first 82 revolutionaries to Sierra Maestra. After the triumph of the revolution, Mario returned to his old job at a brewery, where he was a labor union delegate. Fidel offered him a position in the government, but Mario refused. Fidel then fabricated some charges against him and he was sentenced to 30 years in prison. He served his sentence until his last day, bravely as a *plantado*.

The second of the *plantados* was Eusebio Peñalver Mazorra, a guerilla fighter who spent 29 years in prison. Eusebio was part of the group led by Che Guevara in the mountains of Escambray, in the central part of Cuba. After the so-called "triumph" of the revolution, Fidel Castro's regime offered him a military post with twice the salary that he received while working at a gas station. He rejected it, and in mid-1959, Eusebio and other former guerrillas, who had fought to oust Fulgencio Batista, realized that the communists were taking over the new government and took up arms in the same Escambray Mountains. Fidel, Raúl, and Che, with sound knowledge of how to fight guerrillas, eliminated them as soon as they appeared. The last guerrillas were captured at the end of the decade of 1960. Eusebio, along with others, was one of the first captured in October 1959. The other ringleaders were machine-gunned and buried in a mass grave. Eusebio was told they did not kill him because he was black. He would joke years later that he was alive because in communist Cuba of 1959, "aiming at the bull's-eye" (tiro al blanco) was practiced. Tiro al blanco has a double meaning because blanco is the color white and also the word for bull's-eye. So, when you say "tiro al blanco!" it can mean "hit the bull's-eye" or "shoot those that are white".

Already in prison, he was punished more severely than other prisoners just because he was black, although he never lost his splendid sense of humor. He used to say that his parents had come to Cuba from Spain, and added that his ancestors were "from Negrete." Eusebio Peñalver Mazorra spent two more years in prison than Nelson Mandela. Peña, his nickname, was faithful to his principles, and he was honest and respected by all Cubans who knew him. He is a Cuban martyr of the diaspora.

My uncle José Pujals Mederos was also one of the *Plantados*. He was imprisoned the third-longest period of time, for 27 years and 22 days. He went through 12 different prisons and was transferred 18 times, a technique used by the regime to destabilize political prisoners. My uncle was married to Gloria Lizama Verdeja, back when Cuba was a democracy under a rule of law. My uncle was taught the scale of values, "God, Country and Family," at the Colegio de la Salle, and wanted his future wife to be aware of these values before they got engaged. He was imprisoned years later, in 1961, after the Bay of Pigs invasion. My aunt, who had sent their three children, all under 11 years of age, to the United States, decided to stay in Cuba to visit her husband in prison when it was allowed, which was not very often. In fact, my uncle spent eight years in complete isolation in a windowless cell in the Boniato prison without even so much as a light. During that time, she did not know whether he was alive or dead. In 1988, he was released from prison, thanks to the pressure exerted by a human rights organization. In 1997, at the end of a conference that my uncle gave at the Spanish-Cuban Foundation in Madrid, someone in the audience asked him, "How could you survive so many years in prison?" My uncle pulled out a rosary from the right pocket of his pants. Holding up the rosary, he simply said, "Thanks to my faith in God."

The next *plantado* of the group is Ernesto Díaz Rodríguez, one of the kindest and most loving people I have ever met in my life. He spent more than 22 years in prison. At a young age in Cojímar, a small village near the city of Havana, he helped his father fish for a living, but when the Castro dictatorship took over, he and his family went into exile. Ernesto, feeling uneasy about being in a foreign land, joined the Alpha 66 group and moved to an island in the Bahamas, where he launched invasions into Cuba. Castro's army captured Ernesto in one of his clandestine operations. He remained on a hunger strike for more than 180 days, the last 30 of which he had to be fed intravenously. While in prison, Ernesto read countless books and wrote several works of poetry. In 1992, the Pen Club of Paris interceded and he was released from prison. In exile, he published *Entre Rejas* (Between Bars), in which he recounts his experiences in captivity.

The youngest of the group is Ángel de Fana, one of the few *plantados* still alive and keeping the flame burning in the struggle for the freedom of Cuba. Ángel was well known on the island, because, before joining the *plantados*, he had been the director of Radio CID (Cuba Independiente y Democrática), an organization led by Huber Matos, former commander of the revolution who spent 20 years in prison as a *plantado*.

In order to raise awareness of the dramatic lives of the *plantados*, and their dedication to the freedom of the Cuban people, we are trying to produce a film. The script will have the approval of these men whose experiences will be portrayed in the film. We hired, at first, a renowned, award-winning French screenwriter and director. He met with the *plantados* in a conference room at a Madrid hotel, both individually and as a group. After a week, everyone agreed that he would draft a summary explaining how he would write the script. Once we received the two-page overview, we did not make it past the title, *Hombres Mansos*, meaning "the meek men." According to the screenwriter, he had not seen a shred of hatred in the *plantados* toward Castro and his fellow tyrants. In addition, the screenwriter demanded terms unacceptable to us, stating that in no way he would speak badly of Castro, because the screenwriter had idolized the tyrant during his adolescent years. I remember what my uncle José said, "He does not mind touching the cat's collar, but not the cat."

Needless to say, we dropped the leftist French screenwriter and turned to Hollywood. We looked for a film producer who was both Catholic and ideologically conservative, and we opted for the executive producers of movies such as *Braveheart* and *The Passion of Christ*. We hired an Iranian-born writer, conservative-leaning, who was against any kind of dictatorship. He not only met with the *plantados*, but also with a score of former political prisoners, men and women. I attended all the meetings, and I must admit that all the narratives were shocking. The scriptwriter jotted down detailed notes about the ancient and recent history of Cuba, but a problem arose before we had received the first draft of the script. We drew up a contract very similar to the original one, but under the terms set by the screenwriter, the *plantados* could not review the screenplay. These changes to the contract seemed illogical. Then we received a letter notifying us that the screenwriter had decided to withdraw from the project, because he did not accept anyone intervening in his work.

A year later, the producer introduced me to another scriptwriter, who accepted our terms of the *plantados* being able to review the script. However, we were again unpleasantly surprised when we received the first draft and saw that it was a faithful reflection of the life of Eloy Gutiérrez Menoyo, a man we did not consider a real *plantado*. I finally came to the conclusion that the ultimate scriptwriter must be

Cuban; otherwise he or she cannot understand the principles and behavior of a *plantado*. The film reflecting the life of the plantados is currently one of my unfinished projects.

In September 2002, a group of friends, Gus and Lilliam Machado, Fausto Díaz, and Remedios Díaz Oliver, and I traveled to Washington, DC. During that trip several Cuban-American congressmen and senators highlighted the need for a lobbying group to prevent the U.S. agricultural sector from doing business with the Castro regime. Also on that trip, we met Mauricio Claver-Carone, a young Cuban-American lawyer who advised us that a political action committee (PAC) needed to be created in order to maintain the U.S. embargo on Cuba. The embargo was named under the Helms-Burton law and was to remain in place until basic human rights were respected on the island, political prisoners released, and free and fair elections held.

I proposed that my friends from that DC trip lead the new PAC. Thanks to their work and that of thousands of Cuban-American patriots who have contributed to the PAC, the embargo is still active and effective. Not even Barack Obama has been able to change the law, despite the fact that the Democratic Party had the majority in the House of Representatives and the Senate from 2008 to 2010. In fact, only the very liberal Republicans, in the European sense, or the far-left Democratic Party, are against the famous U.S.-Cuba embargo.

Recently, an Israeli whom I met asked me if I had returned to Cuba after leaving. I answered with another question, "If the Hitler regime had lasted more than 50 years, would you have traveled to Germany?" She lowered her head and, in a low voice, replied, "I understand you."

23

PASSION FOR HORSES: THE CENTURION HORSE FARM

Since my childhood in Cuba, I have dreamed of living on, for, and off the land. I wanted to raise animals or harvest food products on my grandmother's land. Most likely, if Castro's dictatorship had not taken over Cuba, I would have inherited one of my mother's family farms and made a living as an agricultural engineer, a career I would have pursued in college. However, exile quickly ended that dream and my life took a very different path.

When I started making money at TelePizza, I decided to pick up the pieces of my childhood dreams and become involved with farming activities. It was at this time that the Pure Spanish Breed Horse or Caballo de Pura Raza Espanola(PRE) first came into my life. The beauty of these horses immediately caught my eye, but that quickly grew into something much deeper when I learned of their other unique quality: their good temper.

At the beginning of King Philip II's reign in 1560, he ordered the Royal Stables to be built in the city of Córdoba to create a new breed, the PRE horse. Over three generations, royal grooms worked with more than 1,000 mares. King Philip II's goal was to look for a noble animal with a beautiful shape, comprised of a convex head, long neck, thin and arched body, long and rich mane and tail, white coat, and with elevated movements. To that end, he crossed stallions and mares, mostly black, brown, and chestnut, with the few pure white horses that existed at that time. Through this breeding process came what was called the defect of the gray hair. Today 80 percent of this breed are "tordos." These horses are born dark gray or brown and in time they turn white.

Centuries ago, the king who created the PRE horse breed gave them to Spanish noblemen and aristocrats as well as to foreign monarchs and nobles. The Lipizzaner horse of Vienna is a good example because its origins are Spanish. Historically, European countries have developed their own breeds and have made horse sales an important industry. In Holland, there is the KWPN and the Frisian; in Germany, the Hanoverian and Westphalian; in England and Ireland, the English thoroughbred; in France, the Selle Francais; and in Portugal, the Lusitanian. In Spain, the breeding of PRE horses was focused on personal and private enthusiasts rather than becoming an industry. The PRE horse was used for farming rather than for competition, such as classic dressage. I was motivated to breed PRE horses with the intention of improving the breed and hopefully competing against the central European horses in dressage. In the process, I wanted to develop a marketable PRE horse industry in Spain. That is the type of challenge that especially motivates me.

In 1995, during the nine months that I was away from presiding over TelePizza, I bought three fillies and a couple of 3-year-old future stallions. Then I created a stud farm with Luis Carlos Palacios, owner of the Abulense cheese factory, which sold TelePizza most of its mozzarella cheese. He was the one who suggested that we become partners with an expert to proceed with the purchase of fillies and mares to breed them with the best stallions we could find. At that time I did not own a farm, so we kept them on Luis Carlos' property at El Espinar, in the province of Segovia. When I returned to the company in June 1996, I was able to buy a 200-acre farm to keep the animals that we were buying. Then, we learned that the "expert" was manipulating the price of each animal that we were purchasing behind our backs. It was a typical case of corruption and deceit.

Despite the disappointment, I wanted to continue breeding horses in order to create and develop them into specimens capable of competing against the Dutch and German dressage horses. Luis Carlos could not keep up with the pace of my investment in the business. He asked me if I could purchase his share of the horses that we had previously bought together. By then I already had two farms dedicated to the breeding and training of PRE horses. We developed a horse show in the year 2000 and for two years we raised awareness of the Centurion PRE horse.

I was living in the Bahamas with my family, but I had a lot of people dedicated to the breeding operations back in Spain. There was a constant contradiction in their criteria, and finally, I concluded that in order to have a profitable stud farm, we had to raise males and females within the breed that showed a good aptitude and attitude suited for classic dressage. I decided to hire an expert in this field, a Spaniard named Isidro Maldonado, who has a phenomenal track record training young horses and riders to the St. George and Grand Prix level.

Recently, we began working with Javier Cañon, a professor at the University Complutense de Madrid and head of the genetics department as well as a faculty member in the department of veterinary medicine. We are currently conducting a genetics study that will tell us the percentage of heritability of the most important qualities that we wish for the Centurion PRE horses to acquire.

One of the main characteristics of a PRE horse is its temperament, which greatly influences the animal's learning and riding capability. In addition, our horses stand out for their ability to elevate and suspend their front legs. This is essential for piaffe and passage at the Grand Prix level, which is the most demanding in dressage competition. By contrast, the PRE's main drawback is the lack of strength of the hind legs, which affects the trot and gallop of the animal. To correct this deficiency, in recent years we have purchased a number of strong stallions and mares. We are already improving the height and bone structure of the animal, and we must now improve our horses with a great walk. In order to withstand the weight of the rider and the physical pressure to execute the toughest exercises, a larger horse with better pillars is needed. We believe that the height of the Centurion PRE horse should be between 168 and 171 centimeters. With this height, the circumference of the front legs around the knee and the leg should be approximately 37 and 23 centimeters, respectively.

In order to increase the probability of breeding better horses, we have implemented an embryo transfer program. Our mares are split into two groups, the donors and the surrogate mothers. The best females donate two to three embryos, which are inserted into the surrogate mothers, or mares for rent.

With a large recipient mare, meaning a horse with a thoracic perimeter over 200 centimeters that is well fed since early pregnancy, we have produced colts and fillies with a height measuring between 106 and 110 centimeters at birth. Experience has taught us that if feeding continues throughout the first 36 months of their lives, they will measure around 170 centimeters tall and will have the desired bone size. We have noticed that about 64 percent of the foal's growth occurs in the mother's womb, so nutrition during this period is critical.

When the horses are 3 years old, we conduct a very strict selection. We choose the top 30 colts and fillies from each yearly foaling to determine their aptitude and attitude for competing in dressage events. To reach our goal as quickly as possible we aim to produce 250 foals annually from our stock of more than 300 mares. These births are split into approximately 130 embryos from 60 of the best donor mares, which are then gestated by the recipient mares. The remaining balance of 120 comes from pregnant mares that gestate their own foal. We are convinced that after three or four generations, we will establish the necessary qualities to breed future champions in dressage.

One of the farms, San Pedro de las Dueñas, located in the municipality of Lastras del Pozo in Segovia, has 2,500 acres dedicated almost exclusively to the breeding and training of Centurion PRE horses for dressage. At this location, we have implemented an automatic feeding system to provide the appropriate amount of grain for each animal, depending on their size and age. In this way we reduce colics, which is the major cause of death in horses, provoked by eating too much food too quickly.

To date, as far as participation in morphological contests is concerned, we have won first place three times in the Spanish annual championship as best exhibiting breeder. Among many individual awards received, the most noteworthy are the first place in the championship of Spain, awarded to Rondeño IX, and later too Lirona Ram. The two prizes that motivated us the most were the young movement champions of Spain in 2012 and 2013, with two animals born at our Centurion stud farm, Nora Cen and Panacea Cen.

Some time ago, one of my closest collaborators, Perico Español, told me, "Leo, you became rich with TelePizza and famous with Jazztel, but you will always be remembered for the Centurion horse of Pura Raza Española." I hope that proves to be true!

While I would like to say that this new "industry" has been an enormous success, so far horse breeding is a financial bottomless pit. I like to joke that I have been nominated three times for the Nobel Prize in chemistry, because each year these horses convert roughly 18 pounds of gold into 200,000 pounds of horse manure. Due to the costs, most people would have abandoned the project. However, I am determined to improve or correct the flaws in our horses. I am confident that the costs will be recouped and that in my lifetime more than one Centurion PRE horse will compete for the Olympic gold medal in dressage. There is also no doubt that the Centurion PRE will be recognized as one of the world's top horses.

I have also recently taken up the hobby of raising gyrfalcons at my farm. Like horses, the best falcons are prized for their size, speed and beauty. Gyrfalcons are rare and difficult to breed in captivity, a task for which we have a team of qualified professionals. I recently acquired one of the largest breeding stocks in the world, which combined with my existing stock will lead to profitable results. In the next five years it is my forecast that the income derived from the sale of falcons will be so great as to cover the losses from the horse breeding operation. This will make the farm profitable as an enterprise. Once that is achieved, the Centurion Farm may very well become my third Harvard Business Case in the category of how a commercial endeavor can grow out of an altruistic one for the purpose of sustaining the whole.

24

THE MANAGEMENT PHILOSOPHY THAT I HAVE APPLIED TO ACHIEVE MY DREAMS

The basic idea that has always accompanied me in sales efforts is that it is crucial to understand the mentality of the eventual buyer of my product. This is true even in the case of this book. In setting out to write it, I asked a number people what they expected to find, or would like to learn about me, in reading my autobiography. Most of them said that they wanted to understand the key to my "luck," with both TelePizza and Jazztel. My response to this question is that the key to my success was based on the recruiting, training and development of an army of managers. I have always tried to instill the managerial mindset in company personnel, including every human being that is on our payroll. I know that if a person is committed to becoming an expert in their area of responsibility and to forming good habits, they will be a success both for the company and for themselves. They must practice their personal development every day. In doing so, they will progress up the management chain of command, and they will be "intrapreneurs" or entrepreneurs. Their hard work and commitment (what outside commentators love to call "luck") grew some of the biggest companies in Spain.

ACQUIRING THE APPROPRIATE HABITS

The first thing I recommend is that everyone should understand the importance of good habits and the repercussions of bad ones. Previously I discussed how Benjamin Franklin educated himself and worked to attain the virtues he desired in life. Thanks to his autobiography, I discovered the value of being self-taught. The points that follow explain where good habits come from and what emerges from them. Any habit starts with a thought, and that thought makes us develop ideas that we repeat to ourselves and discuss with the people around us.

From there:

1. Listen to suggestions to enrich or to help develop that idea. At this point it is essential to have constructive creativity and a high level of motivation.

2. Follow a defined action plan. I must admit that I have met many people who, being unable to achieve their dreams, try to discourage others, instead of stimulating them.

Then, of course, action must be taken. This is where fear plays an important role. The continual repetition of an action and implementing the planned strategy allow us to acquire good or bad habits (figure 24.1). Those habits will shape our character and will largely dictate our destiny.

Figure 24.1 – Formation of a Thought into Action

In this regard, there are phrases that have been repeated to me since childhood, phrases that I will never forget. For example, my father used to say, *"El hábito no hace al monje, pero sí al hombre."* This is a play on the word *hábito*, which means both "habit" and also can be used to describe the robe of a monk. It means: "Because the monk wears a robe, it does not mean he behaves as a monk". A human being's character is defined by his habits, his personal behavior. It does not matter what your family background is, or the organization to which you belong. All that matters are the habits that have been acquired throughout one's lifetime. Bosses are not made by the way they dress, how big their office is, or whether or not they have a personal secretary. A leader must provide guidance, support and must know how to sell ideas. Leaders earn the respect of his or her employees and teach them the strategies that need to be implemented in the business plan.

Another phrase that comes to mind is one that I learned from my great-aunt, that: "Life is too short to afford the luxury of acquiring bad habits." Lazy people have acquired bad habits during childhood that accompany them throughout their entire lives (laziness being chief amongst them).

Nevertheless, one of the most important expressions that struck me like a lightning bolt the first time I read it is one attributed to General George S. Patton Jr.: "Ninety percent of humanity dies at age 40 and are buried at 70." It is essential to continue with self-improvement in order to eliminate the bad habits that make us swim against the tide. Bad habits do not allow us to make progress, prevent us from moving forward, and make most people give up.

In my opinion, an individual's life can be divided into five 20-year stages:

1. In the early years of our lives we tend to live under the wings of our parents, and they dictate almost everything we do and learn. During the adolescent years, we begin to show that we want something different, which is why so many youngsters become rebels, with or without a cause.

2. From 20-40 years of age is the critical period in which we must define our goals within our chosen field. In addition to becoming an expert and acquiring good habits, we must read, learn and practice every aspect of our profession. In doing so we will become self-reliant, which is essential if we wish to achieve our dreams.

3. When we are around 40 years old, we make use of everything that we have learned and it is around this time that we should be prepared to enjoy the journey to fulfill our dreams. However, I insist once again, it is *fundamental* to acquire good habits, avoiding *fearitis* and *excusitis*, of which I spoke earlier, that always threaten to paralyze us. To that end, action, discipline, and willpower are essential.

4. Between the ages of 60 and 80, we must concentrate on transmitting our experience and acquired knowledge to younger generations. It is also the stage, after entrepreneurial success, when we focus on altruistic projects to leave behind a footprint or footprints cast in stone for the betterment of society.

5. If we live past 80 years of age, in addition to considering ourselves fortunate for living so long, we should feel fulfilled and satisfied by having seen our dreams come true before closing the eyes that God gave us for the last time.

THE HABIT OF THE THOUGHT PROCESS: FROM VISION TO STRUCTURE

Another lesson I try to convey is the importance of acquiring the habit of the thought process, from Vision to Structure, that I have acquired over the years (figure 24.2). I have developed my own concoction after reading dozens of books that offer different explanations, concepts, and vocabulary, but also from the experiences during my professional career and the creation of TelePizza. This thought process applies not just to individuals but to any organization, family, business, government entity, or foundation.

Figure 24.2 – The Thought Process: From Vision to Structure

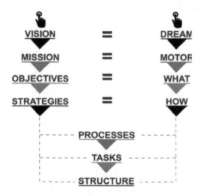

Before explaining what the thought process is, I would like to mention another of the phrases that has inspired me. I do not know anyone who has arrived where he wanted to go without knowing beforehand where he was going.

The first step in the process is to identify your Vision. So I always explain that in the same way that a person has a dream or aspirations, a company should have a Vision to know what they want to achieve.

I often tell my team to imagine that they are in a desert dying of thirst and hunger after several days without eating or drinking. At one point they see, far away, an oasis. Then the Vision should be, "We have to reach that oasis before we die!"

The requirements in defining a Vision are:

1. To define the business and clarify our area of involvement: "Who is our customer, where are we, and when will we get there?"

2 To be beneficial to all team members.

3. To be extraordinary. This is the "star" that you or your company should be shooting for!

4. To be measurable and able to answer the question, "What is to be achieved and when?" Your measurements and benchmarks should take progress into account.

5. To be motivational and empowering to the whole team. They must want to achieve the vision above any other consideration.

6. To be concise.

7. To be "sellable" and "achievable". Other team/family members must agree and believe in order to make it a reality. *Fearitis* and *Excusitis* will kill your Vision if you are not surrounded by believers. Those that are not convinced must be replaced, or in the case of family members, placed (delicately) on the sidelines.

8. To be revisable over time. As time passes you are getting closer to the destination. A Vision should be three to five years away; as you approach your completion date you must refresh your Vision!

9. To ensure compatibility between the personal and professional Visions.

If your Vision is missing any of these elements, you should review your thought process to ensure that every nut and bolt is included in the machinery. Otherwise problems could appear later.

Once the Vision has been defined, we must identify the phrase that we should repeat to ourselves every day to achieve it. This is what I call the motor, or Mission. For example, on a football team, the Mission would be: "We must win."

At TelePizza, we said, "We must grow." The following are the five requirements of every Mission:

1. It must be the reason or purpose of the entity's existence.

2. It must be the motor that motivates and unites the team so that everyone is moving in the same direction.

3. It should help set the basic Objectives on which the survival and perpetuation of the enterprise depends.

4. It should be achievable but never ending.

5. It should help in making difficult decisions. Ask the questions: If we do what is being proposed, is it going to enhance our Mission or help us to achieve it? If we do not do it, is it going to hinder us in fulfilling our Mission?

Having identified the Mission, the next step is to identify the key Objectives on which the survival and perpetuation of the business depend. These derive from the question, what needs to be accomplished in each of the key areas of the enterprise?

These key areas are:

1. Top Management

2. Marketing

3. Innovation

4. Human Resources

5. Physical Resources

6. Finance

7. Contributions to Society

8. Profitability

Each Objective must be:

1. Beneficial, contributing to achieving the Mission.

2. Measurable, the answer to "what to do and when." If it is not measurable, the Objective would be debatable, or subjective.

3. Challenging, and serving as a motivator.

4. Achievable, so we do not become discouraged.

5. Agreed upon by the parties involved.

Once each Objective has been defined, it is time to use our constructive creativity and ask ourselves, how can we achieve it? Thus we will define Strategies, breaking them down into Processes and Tasks.

Of course, if it were that easy, everyone would succeed in life and fulfill their dreams, all businesses would make a lot of money and government bureaucracies would function like a Swiss watch. However, there are only three resources in this world: the human, the physical, and the financial. The lack of any one of them would force us to ask ourselves, "Which came first, the chicken or the egg?" For example, there were occasions during which TelePizza had the money but not the locations to open stores. Other times, we had the store sites but did not have the trained personnel to operate the stores, or lacked the money for construction. At this point the excuses usually appear, but what we really need to do is to redefine the Objectives and Strategies. My priority has always been growth in sales, because the most important Objective of any business is to increase sales and, therefore, I have never accepted an excuse to prevent us from growing the top line of our income statement (figure 24.3).

Figure 24.3

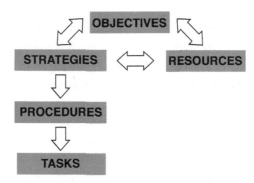

The following anecdote further illustrates the Thought Process from Vision to Structure:

A sociologist was commissioned to study the mentality of different people working on a construction site. He approached a bricklayer, who was kneeling, laying bricks with mortar as he was building a wall, and asked him:

"What are you doing here?"

"You cannot see?" answered the bricklayer. He continued, "I wake up at 5:30 AM and arrive at work at 7 AM, which is the time that I am supposed to start working. I have to lay bricks to build this wall until 4 PM, following the instructions of the foreman. We are entitled to a 20-minute coffee break in the morning and an hour for lunch. I earn 10 dollars per hour, but if I work overtime, they pay me time and a half, and if I work on Sunday, they pay me double."

The bricklayer is performing tasks. In reference to Chart 24.2 these tasks flow from the Vision, Mission, Strategies or Processes laid out by others. (See Figure 24.2).

The sociologist continued walking around the work site, where he met the foreman, who was talking to a number of workers. He raised the same question:

"What are you doing here?"

"Well, look," said the foreman. "I am responsible for all my workers fulfilling their tasks. I have to coordinate them so that they comply with the architect's assistant's instructions given to me. If I get them to finish everything correctly and on time, I will get paid 20 percent more, in addition to my salary."

The foreman is involved in implementing the Strategies, Processes and Tasks which stem from the Vision, Mission and Objectives. (See: Figure 24.2).

The sociologist continued walking around the building site and met the architect's assistant. He was surrounded by a lot of architectural drawings on the table and was talking to a foreman.

"What are you doing here?"

"My responsibility in this job," he said, "is to ensure that by the end of September, before the rains start, we will have finished the building. For this to happen, every week I meet with the job specialty managers to agree on what we should do within the building, depending on their expertise. Furthermore, I coordinate the orders for the materials needed to carry out the work without causing delays. Every day I meet with the foreman to monitor the compliance with the deadlines, as well as to verify that the hours and the materials needed to continue with the project are within the budget. If I finish on or before the agreed upon deadline, I will receive a 30 percent bonus, in addition to my salary."

Therefore, the architect's assistant is responsible to meet the work Objectives and to agree with the foremen about the right Strategies to ensure that they comply with their action plan. (See: Figure 24.2). These are defined from the Vision and Mission.

When the sociologist left the construction site, he met a very well-dressed man with a helmet like the rest of the workers. The sociologist asks:

"What are you doing here?"

"I am building a cathedral. I verify that the building is being erected according to my architectural drawings."

The architect, within this example, is responsible for defining the dream and surrounds himself with the necessary professionals to ensure the fulfillment of his Vision. There are four different characters with four different mentalities. As I often say, *"Hay de todo en la viña del Señor." There is a little of everything in God's grove.*

I must stress the importance of the proper implementation of all the tasks, on time and correctly. If one of them is not properly fulfilled, it is almost certain that the completion of the process will be affected. This produces a domino effect in which the completion of the action plan, the objectives, and the mission would be hindered.

The enterprise structure, or the company's organizational chart, is defined by the number of tasks that are included in the strategies. The structure should be as horizontal as possible, so that the upper echelons of the company are as close as possible to the employee that deals directly with the customer.

The knowledge and experiences that have helped me so much in achieving my entrepreneurial success are as follows:

- The accounting and financial knowledge learned in my university studies.

- The training in personnel management and military discipline acquired while I attended Officer Candidate School in the U.S. Army.

- Having learned to sell ideas to employees, suppliers, bosses, and customers at Kirby Vacuum Cleaners, Procter & Gamble, and Johnson & Johnson.

- Identifying, developing, and acquiring habits that have helped me swim with the current of the river of life instead of against it.

- All the managerial knowledge learned from the books I read, thanks to the perseverance of my father.

- Common sense, which is the least common of all senses. This exists only when one is not selfish and, above all, thinks of the common good, inside and outside the organization. I have come to define common sense as applying logic with the absence of the seven deadly sins (wrath, greed, sloth, pride, lust, envy, and gluttony).

- Finally, I cannot forget about the Ethical Values taught to me by my parents at home, since my early childhood.

The Management Cycle

Figure 24.4 – The Successful Habits of a Manager

In one of Peter Drucker's books, he writes that any person holding a job in a company or organization must behave as a manager in the workplace. The role of each manager is to increase productivity in his area. It is applicable to all employees of every company, from the cleaning staff to the President.

To be a manager one must practice the Management Cycle, which begins the night before going to work. One must identify the Objectives one wishes to achieve the following day. Once they are defined, one should plan everything that has to be done to comply with the Objectives and, in turn, be organized in order to be as efficient as possible. During the day one executes the work plan and once it is done, one measures whether the Objectives were achieved or not. After the measurement, one must analyze the results. If one has accomplished them, why? And if not, why not? After arriving at the appropriate conclusions, one will make the necessary modifications and will practice the management cycle every night and day of the year.

At this point it seems pertinent to note the difference between being effective and efficient, and for this I will relate to you another story. A passenger in an aircraft hears a message from the pilot. "Good morning, this is the captain speaking. I have good news and bad news. First, the good news is that we are flying at high speed. The bad news is that we do not know where we are going, because the compass is broken."

This is a perfect case in which the good news highlights the efficiency and the bad news highlights the lack of effectiveness. In business it is essential to do the proper thing the first time and afterward to repeat it efficiently. Unfortunately, not everyone does the first things right, and some do not continue maintaining the same quality. I have met on more than one occasion those whom I have labeled "idiots with initiative." Those who know me well have heard me exclaim: "Thank goodness this person is not a centipede!" By this I mean most idiots only put one foot in their mouth. Centipedes have 100 feet.

Figure 24.4 shows the cycle of successful management habits, and there is a box labeled "constructive creativity," which is essential for identifying and defining the Strategies necessary to achieve the Objectives. I have always said that if you do not find the solutions to the problems that have arisen during the day, it is best to go to sleep thinking about how to solve the problems. In the U.S. Army I learned that the human body needs just a few hours of sleep to rest, but that is not the case with the brain, which needs even less sleep. That is why sometimes you wake up at midnight with a solution to a problem that previously seemed unsolvable. The next step is to start all over again, i.e., to plan again the next day to modify what did not go as it should have.

The Constructive Mentality

Figure 24.5 Constructive Versus Destructive Mindsets

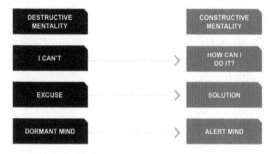

In figure 24.5, two different types of mentalities are compared. In the left column is the destructive mentality, and in the right the constructive mindset. A company, like everything else in life, works just like the employees think and act. The difference between companies that are successful and those that are not depends on the percentage of people who have the destructive versus the constructive mentality.

Management Training

Something that is not often taught is how to become a competent boss. We often hear about the importance of the practice of medicine or law, but not the training of leaders. Many say that a leader is born and not made. In my opinion, leadership requires training! At a minimum, this should include sales techniques to persuade people and training to speak in public to motivate an audience. People should be conditioned to *Think Big* and to follow the Thought Process from Vision to Structure. The daily exercise of the Management Cycle should be re-enforced and practiced as second nature.

To ensure the growth of companies where I have worked or that I have created, I have always been personally involved in the training of executives and those aspiring to become one. Therefore, my companies have given theoretical and practical training in the following management skills:

1. Defining the Vision of the entity to include thinking big and shooting for the stars.

2. Providing guidance and support to your subordinates in order to increase their productivity continually.

3. Personally practicing the Management Cycle on a daily basis.

4. Learning how to sell ideas in order to communicate well.

5. Selecting your team after the Human Resources department has provided valid candidates.

6. Elaborating an action plan, which should be the result of the Strategies agreed upon with your subordinate, who should, at the same time, reach a consensus with his team.

7. Training and motivating one's team of between five and eight people, dedicating the necessary time to each of them.

8. Evaluating and measuring results in an objective manner.

9. Helping to develop subordinates through guidance and support so that they can be future competent managers, and trying to have at all times two or three candidates who could replace you.

Figure 24.6 Attributes of a Boss

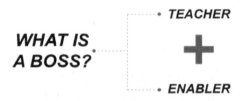

When a boss does not sleep because an employee is not fulfilling his or her responsibilities he must let that employee know, without making a threat, and report the incident or behavior to the Human Resources department. If the employee does not correct their improper behavior, a second notice should be given, and if there is a third incident, the employee should be dismissed. My philosophy is in accordance with the following: "For the ones who do not know, you teach them. For the ones who lack the means, you provide them with the means and resources. Lastly, for those who do not want or who do not comply in fulfilling their Objectives, you invite them to leave the company, pointing out that they will probably be happier elsewhere."

10. Make the right decisions on time, and if the situation requires it, be able to change the decision.

- We must learn to conduct an ongoing analysis of the strategies, processes, and tasks of the business plan in order to determine their effectiveness.
- If the strategies need a radical change, and an executive has to to make a 180-degree change in direction, he or she must make the decision and sell the idea to the entire team.

11. Finally, maintaining correct ethical principles.

THE SALE OF IDEAS

First of all, sales is a poorly understood and misinterpreted activity. Nearly everyone associates it with the sales profession, not realizing that every day, from the moment we wake up, every person is selling (many poorly) something all day long. In a family, the parents should sell their children on good behavior, the importance of studying, etc. The parents try to convince each other of the activities that their children should be involved in, how to educate them, where to go on vacation, which restaurant to go to for dinner, and what car or house to buy. When we go to our workplace, we are in the position of having to convince our bosses, our employees, or our own coworkers of any number of things. I wonder: is this not selling? If so, why is it that when one graduates from college, there is a celebration, but when one gets their first job as a salesperson it is not worthy of celebration? In my opinion it is the most important profession in the world. Sales is a skill we must all learn because the ability to sell makes the world a better place. So my advice is that everyone should be proud of being a successful salesperson. Many top executives who have been promoted to senior management positions without knowing how to sell do not dare take a sales course, because they do not want to tarnish their ego or image. I encourage those executives to leave their comfort zone, even if it hurts their pride a little, because in the medium and long terms they will be much more productive and self-confident.

I have often heard people say that like leaders, a salesperson is born, not made. I think this is the point of view of many who are not involved in selling. It describes naturally nice, outgoing, talkative, and funny people. However, there are also shy, introverted, and much quieter people, and these qualities could make them think that they would not succeed as salesmen. From my experience I can say that through the continued practice of selling techniques anyone can become a competent salesperson, no matter their personality type. This is true not only in the selling of products, but also ideas, especially if sales techniques are learned at an early age.

I believe so much in the importance of selling ideas that all TelePizza store managers and employees who supervised personnel took three courses on sales techniques and then they taught the fourth course to their own subordinates. Some people have taken a sales course and believe that they already know it all. It is like when someone tells a joke and some people think they know it, but actually, they do not know how to tell it. Sales techniques must be practiced in the correct sequence until they become habits. These techniques should be natural, involuntary. Some of the most common errors or mistakes in selling are the following:

1. Not knowing what you are selling and who the decision maker approving the purchase is. For example, I have seen salesmen who went into a hospital without defining the product or the department that should be targeted, nor planning a strategy for introducing it. I have also seen executives unable to define the responsibilities of their subordinates.

2. Another common error is not creating a pleasant atmosphere with the person to whom you have to sell a product or an idea. Without achieving a pleasant atmosphere you may create an uncomfortable situation that may hinder making the sale.

3. Many salesmen rush to talk about the product regardless of other considerations, such as customer needs and the product features and benefits. So I always say that you have to sell the "sizzle, not the steak." Many salesmen put the steak right on the table and ask "Do you want this steak?" The better way is to understand the customer's needs and present characteristics and benefits that meet those needs before presenting the product. If you present the sound of the meat crackling on the grill and explain how the incredible aroma is the result of superior marbling and proper aging, while the unique preparation is designed to ensure the most delicious and satisfying celebration one can have in a restaurant – believe me, they'll be hungry for steak! The point is: before talking about an idea or a product, we must obtain information from the customer about what his needs are.

4. Sometimes salesmen have excessive pressure on their shoulders. I usually advise them to imagine themselves as Santa Claus with a red sack full of gifts that the customer wants. This helps to take the pressure off the salesmen.

5. A common mistake is not listening to the customer. God gave us two ears and one mouth to listen twice as much as we speak, but often we insist on doing the opposite.

6. Frequently, the salesperson does not dare to close the sale or get a commitment to buy from the customer. When closing a sale, I do not recommend asking a question if the answer would be yes or no. I recommend offering alternatives, so that the customer feels that he is choosing and whatever the outcome, one always wins.

7. It is essential to know to keep silent after asking a question. The first one that speaks is the one that loses.

8. It is advisable to maintain eye contact with your customer at all times.

DESIGN OF A COMPANY STRUCTURE

In all the organizations that I have managed I always have implemented the organizational chart with the inverted pyramid, in which the base is the top and the tip is the base, contrary to what often happens in almost all organizations, in which the structure forces employees to think that their boss is the most important individual. I have always told my employees that the most important person in the company is the customer, next the employees who deal directly with the customer and then, lastly, the President. The whole structure must be geared toward helping employees who are closest to the customers in order to keep them satisfied. The message to everyone in the company is to face the customer, with your back to the boss.

Figure 24.7 Traditional Versus Ideal Corporate Structures

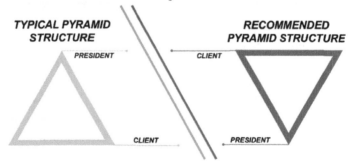

As the company's sales grow, the number of defined tasks in the business plan increases. A lack of personnel will be noticed when, among other reasons, the different heads in the organizational chart are in the following situations:

1. When you realize you do not have enough time to do everything that is in your area of responsibility to meet the business plan.

2. When the boss lacks the technical knowledge on any subject, it will be more profitable to hire an expert.

I have come across many situations where outside experts are needed to resolve a problem due to of the lack of personnel or technical knowledge. Once the job is done, the external services should end. More than once, I have had to ask why we continued using a service provider after the initial issue was resolved. I have heard in response: "just because," "because I say so," or "because that is the way it is." This is a costly, and unfortunate manner of thinking.

One story that comes to mind and that reflects this situation is the story of the green bench.

Years ago, military installations were commanded by a colonel and would normally be visited by the general once or twice a year. It was common practice to paint all the buildings with their typical colors, green and white, before the general's visit. In one of these military installations, 30 years ago, the colonel ordered that all of the facilities be painted and, observing that there was a freshly painted green bench, he ordered that a guard be placed next to the bench, so that nobody would sit on it and have his clothes stained green. Time passed and, years later, there was another colonel in charge of the military installations. During his visit he went by the green bench and noticed that there was a guard. "What is this soldier doing here?" he asked. The major said, "Colonel, he has always been here, at least since I came two years ago," to which the colonel answered, "I did not ask if he has always been here, but what he is doing here."

One word to the wise is enough. At a certain time, maybe a decision made sense, but later on it is no longer necessary or appropriate. Therefore, it is crucial to perform continual analysis of responsibilities, because in that way you can reduce expenses and the company investments.

I am of the opinion that, before offering a job to a person, the job description must be well defined. Among other things, it should be clear who that employee will report to and which goals he will be expected to achieve. I have always stressed the importance of hiring the best employees because, as I say, if you surround yourself with stars, you will shine, and if you surround yourself with mud, you will get muddy.

THE BOARD OF DIRECTORS

If the head of an organization fails, the body will suffer. There are many reasons why the head, or Chairman of the Board, may not perform duties as they should. It could be from unethical behavior, that the person lacks adequate knowledge and experience, has a conflict of interest, or simply be a result of being overly ambitious. The Chairman of the Board must be surrounded by an adequate number of independent directors. Each one must contribute his or her own knowledge and experience learned in different areas of business and should participate in various committees, such as audit and remuneration.

The *Serpico* film, based on true events, is about corruption within the police force of the city of New York. In the film, one person with ethics stands out among all the other officers and chiefs, who were all receiving bribes.

A few years ago I was surprised by the multinational company, Enron. Its President, along with some of the members of the Board of Directors, were accused of falsifying annual financial statements. These were presented to the financial market after being audited by the firm Arthur Andersen, a firm that went bankrupt for being an accomplice to the crime. These two examples have pushed me to emphasize that all board members must get into the guts of the business in their areas of responsibility to ensure that the Strategies, Processes, and Tasks are being implemented properly. Also, I have always insisted on having one or more internal auditors. These auditors must report directly to the Chairman of the Audit Committee, in order to ensure the proper operation of the company.

Recently, I was pleasantly surprised when the Spanish government formally recommended that a percentage of employees, executives, and/or members of the Board of Directors be female. Women are not adequately represented in the different echelons in large companies. I suppose this is due to what the current male executives had learned from their parents. I was lucky to grow up in a home where both my father and my mother prospered in their professions, so it has always been natural for women to work in upper echelon professions at my companies. I think it is not only advisable, but essential, to have women participate on the Board of Directors. In addition to having equal qualifications, women are often more sensible and responsive to the needs of customers. It is also worth noting that the trend in many countries, including the United States, is that more women are graduating with college degrees than men. Women are also earning a greater number of advanced degrees. Any business that does not embrace female leadership will miss out on incredible talent!

I am a firm believer in the right to freedom of thought, expression, and behavior in a government under the rule of law. Based on my experience as a Cuban, I prefer evolution to revolution. I am convinced that as more women work, achieve high positions and set an example, the mentality of society is evolving. Today, the number of female CEO's is increasing, but it is still noteworthy when a female takes the reigns of a company. Soon, seeing a woman occupying a position of power will no longer be seen as exceptional.

From left to right, *Plantados* (political prisoners) Mario Chanes de Armas (a political prisoner who spent 30 years in Castro's prisons), Ernesto Díaz Rodríguez (22+ years) and Eusebio Peñalver Mazorra (29 years). This was taken at a conference describing life under the totalitarian regime in Cuba.

From left to right the *Plantados* Ángel de Fana (a political prisoner who spent 20 years, plus 8 months in Castro's prisons), my Uncle, José Pujals Mederos (27 years) and Ernesto Díaz Rodríguez (22+ years).

Cubans gathering in Miami advocating for the freedom of political prisoners, without forced exile.

Photo of my three young sons with
Rondeño IX.

With Marilina and Rondeño IX.

With professional golfer Seve Ballesteros at the 2005 Spanish Golf Open.

With my friend and golfing partner Fernando Vega-Penichet, celebrating our win in the Sugar Open at Casa de Campo.

With Gonzalo Fernández Castaño and Carlos Suneson, the Professional Golfers sponsored by Jazztel.

My Lambda Chi Alpha fraternity brothers and friends from Stetson University, 40 years after graduation. From left to right: Michael Egan, Robert Kimble, Timothy Thompson and Douglas Danser.

Celebrating New Year's Eve in Miami with my wife Marilina and Gus and Lilian Machado.

At the same New Year's Eve party with Eddie Blanco (far left), Pepe Sánchez and José Ortiz
on the right.

With my childhood friends from Cuba on the first tee. From left: Eddy Sardinas, Agustin
Arellano and Alfonso Cueto, whom we call 'Proton'.

Nine of the eleven cousins of the Pujals family, after forty years in exile. From left to right: Isabel and Graciela Pujals, Genaro Carlos and Leopoldo Fernández Pujals, Alicia and Maria Elena Mora Pujals, Eduardo Fernández Pujals, Victor Pujals and Raúl Mora Pujals.

My son Alejandro at the house we bought in Deland, Florida when I returned from Vietnam and finished my college degree at Stetson University.

My son Carlos at 18 months old in Panama, where we lived during my Johnson & Johnson years.

At the Villafranca house in the northern part of Madrid. From left to right: my oldest son, Alejandro, my father, his wife Catherine and my second son Carlos.

My wife Marilina and I.

My son Carlos, his wife Asiya and my wife Marilina in the cloister at the monastery.

Summer vacation in Venice, Italy in 2002 with my three youngest children Alfonso, Andres and Alberto (left to right).

In the back of our home, the Yellow House, in Lyford Cay, Bahamas with all five of my children, Marilina and my daughter in law Maria Daly Centurion.

At Carlos' wedding celebration with his brother Alejandro.

Dressed up for a night out with Marilina and our three children Alberto, Andres and Alfonso.

Happy times with my eldest sons and two of my grandchildren. Carlos and his son Alex are on the left. To the right of me is my son Alejandro and his daughter, Alessandra.

25

CURRENT AND FUTURE PROJECTS

As I have explained, I firmly believe that life is divided into five different stages. I am now in the fourth stage, in the period from 60 to 80 years old. I remember during Christmas 2012, my wife asked my five children and my two daughters-in-law to define themselves in one word. After all of them had answered, one of my daughters-in-law asked me what word I would use to describe myself. I replied, "Until recently I had defined myself as a 'catalyst', but now I have changed. The word that defines my behavior now is 'focus'. In other words, I am focused on my Objectives."

Everyone looked at me and asked the reason for the change, to which I replied, "Until now I would get involved in new projects, and wherever I have been, I have provoked reactions, as a catalyst does in a chemical laboratory. I have always tried to make sure that the reactions were positive and constructive. I no longer have that need. Now I have another need, and I define myself as 'focused' because, being 65 years old, I must concentrate and focus all my time, efforts and attention on fulfilling my remaining goals. I do not wish for what time I have left in this world to be spent answering the requests of others, attending to things that are their priority, not mine. These requests would take up the time that I need to fulfill my goals. I would not like to reach my 80th birthday, find out I have Alzheimer's and, because I was not focused, leave some dreams unfulfilled."

Of course, everyone at that dinner wanted to know what those dreams were. Almost all the projects in which I am involved are in the same direction. I wish to see my children being self-reliant and able to become achievers in their chosen fields. Also, I would like to have the peace of mind of having passed on to them as many lessons that I have learned along the way during my life as possible.

One of these projects is to write this autobiography, which has four purposes. The first one is to pass on to my children, grandchildren, and future generations the knowledge I have acquired over the years. I want them to understand how the family wealth was created, to appreciate it, respect it, and to know how to use it properly. My hope is that they will increase it and help their descendants and society.

The second purpose is to explain to parents like me everything that my parents taught me. I want other parents to know how much these lessons have helped me to succeed in life, so they can help their children achieve their dreams.

The third purpose is to provide young people with an example so that they can be inspired to succeed in life and to make their dreams come true.

Last but not least, I wish to convey to businessmen and businesswomen the conviction that with hard work, principles, self-training, good habits and a proper managerial mindset that any business can be more productive and much larger than what they might have thought. I also want to explain how to manage it in a more enjoyable manner.

Another endeavor that I have envisioned is working with my children as a consultant or advisor in those professional or entrepreneurial ventures that they wish to carry out. I will convey suggestions, thinking out loud so they make the right decisions. For example, my oldest son Alejandro is a neurologist and has his own practice in the United States. I try to help him to be more productive in his profession. I must say that he is a wonderful person and a great doctor with an incredible reputation for excellence. He is raising a beautiful family and it makes me very proud to see love and unity between generations of family members.

My son Carlos earned a masters degree in hotel and restaurant management after graduating from college. We are collaborating on a number of projects and having a lot of success and fun. At age 37, he is showing personal and professional maturity out of the ordinary and he has already created two popular and fast growing restaurant chains. His first restaurant concept is a gastrobar serving traditional Spanish tapas and proper cocktails. So far, he has opened three Spanish restaurants and will soon announce expansion to several new markets in the United States. His second restaurant concept serves high-end Peruvian cuisine, traditional ceviche and proper cocktails including delicious Pisco Sours. Carlos has opened two Peruvian restaurants and will soon announce that he has broken ground on two more. I get a lot of satisfaction watching him overcome many of the same challenges I encountered growing Telepizza and Jazztel. Opening restaurants is not easy and rapid growth of complex enterprises requires constant re-evaluation of the mission to ensure that the proper capital, human and physical resources are deployed to maximize success. As I mentioned earlier, even when a business is well capitalized, its growth will be limited if it cannot find new locations or train skilled personnel to maintain quality fast enough. He is managing the restaurant growth beautifully and is now beginning to experience the founder role changes explained by Wilson Harrell in *Total Quality Entrepreneurship*. As his enterprises expand, he must increasingly find and rely on skilled managers to make decisions and perform tasks that he once enjoyed.

My son Alberto, who is 22 years old, recently graduated from Babson College, a prestigious institution with a reputation for excellence in marketing and entrepreneurship. He is hard working and very creative, with a passion for music. I think he will be incredibly successful as he is already beginning to show flashes of entrepreneurship. After working in event marketing post-graduation he was able to save enough money to purchase a wide array of sound equipment and staging, and is in the process of setting up a live music business. In addition, he has formed a group of musicians who are writing songs in preparation for a recording album. It is very exciting for me to see my children pursuing their dreams.

Andrés has begun his third year in college, and is committed to completing his studies in accounting and finance. In addition, he is a member of his university's golf team and has made great improvements to his game in a very short period of time. This is a particularly remarkable accomplishment because he set his mind to making a division one golf team while he was already *in college*. In doing so, he demonstrated unusual focus and perseverance putting in many hard hours to improve his conditioning, following a strict diet and training from the wee hours into the night to shave strokes off his score. This type of repetitive and often thankless effort at self-improvement can only come from within. I am proud of his effort and I am sure he will succeed in anything he sets his mind to by following this same formula.

My youngest son, Alfonso, has finished high school and is applying to different universities in the United States. Alfonso is interested in technology and software, and has recently taken up painting. He is another one of my children who has shown highly creative characteristics from an early age and wishes to become successful in business. It is exciting to watch him explore his interests and grow as a young man. It gives me great satisfaction to think about the things he will do in the future to achieve his dreams.

A third project is to organize the transfer of my assets in an orderly fashion. In 2013, my wife and I attended a seminar held by Heinrich Von Liechtenstein, professor at IESE in Barcelona. The topic of the seminar was the importance of families finding the proper way to pass on values from generation to generation in a well-planned and orderly way. That seminar opened both our minds, and we intend to implement these ideas.

My entire family gets together twice a year. Once during the summer and the other to celebrate every New Year. Past gatherings focused on tourism and entertainment. During the Christmas holiday in 2013, for the first time, we held meetings for about two hours a day to begin discussing how to transfer my assets in an orderly fashion.

The meetings covered three topics. One of them is the outline of my management philosophy. I have trained countless executives but I never explained it to my children in detail. The second topic was sales techniques. I am convinced that if I had not acquired that knowledge, I would not have been as successful in my career. I enjoy passing on this knowledge and we have a lot of fun with the classes. Learning is serious but it does not need to be done without humor and camaraderie! The third issue was the reading of the book entitled *Strategy for the Wealthy Family*, by Mark Haynes Daniell, and we have read the first 200 pages and we will continue reading it at future family gatherings. I am sure that it will help us define the family governance protocol. These new endeavors are a sort of declaration of intent, agreed upon by all members of the family, aimed at the successful continuity of the family enterprise by regulating the drive and dedication of the members of the family in their business activities.

The fourth pending project is to turn the Centurion PRE Horse Farm to profitability and leave this world knowing that the Centurion PRE horse will endure the passage of time. To help make the farm profitable, we have recently started a project of breeding white, black and grey gyrfalcons. I am convinced that between the sale of trained horses capable of competing at the Grand Prix level of dressage and the sale of gyrfalcons in the Arabian market, the Centurion PRE Horse Farm will continue in perpetuity.

I have also long intended to establish a chair for entrepreneurs in one of the major universities, where everything that I think an entrepreneur or a senior executive should know would be taught. Along these lines, I have made commitments and intend to establish the Centurion Sales Excellence Program at

Stetson University, which will offer both a major and a minor in sales at the Business School.

Recently my daughter-in-law Maria, Alejandro's wife, reminded me of an anecdote that surprised her, in which she said that a guest was having dinner at our home and she began to tell what she was doing with her business. I began to highlight the pros and cons of what I was hearing and foreseeing. She said that I ended up outlining a brilliant business strategy that helped her. I thoroughly enjoy using my creativity and knowledge to help others and would love to transmit this knowledge to future generations through the Centurion Sales Excellence Program.

Also, as I mentioned in chapter 22, I have a pending film production about the *Plantados*. I hope that young people, upon seeing the movie, will be emotionally touched by their suffering and inspired by their unbreakable principles.

Last but not least, I will always be willing to help rebuild the country where I was born, Cuba. The last period in which the rule of law governed the Republic of Cuba was under the constitution adopted in 1940. Castro imposed a new constitution in 1975 and currently there are a number of people that advocate amending that document to try to establish more freedom in Cuba. I oppose these efforts and believe Castro's laws should be eradicated and totally replaced. I foresee that freedom and liberty will return once again and the rule of law will be restored.

Many Spaniards ask me if I would go back to Cuba when the Castro brothers die, and I always answer that the problem of Cuba is not just the Castros, but the communist regime imposed by them. I remind them that in the Soviet Union, under communism in the last century, the dictator Josef Stalin died in 1953 and it was 35 years later that communism was finally buried. I pray to God and my guardian angel, who has always protected me, to help the Cuban people live in a free and sovereign Cuba.

EPILOGUE
LEOPOLDO'S DREAM: FREEDOM IN CUBA

BY RAÚL RIVERO

A fundamental piece of the awful totalitarianism puzzle is the powerful propaganda machine. While pre-Castro Cuba was truly and honestly thriving financially, with productive sugar fields and a high national income, Castro's propaganda machine managed to paint a false portrait of a failing island in the 1950s, depicting one that was poor and without a future. Simultaneously, Fidel Castro and his brother Raúl, topped off this lie with another: the deceitful idea that Cuba was actually benefiting and progressing while under their strict control.

The Cuban dictatorship had all the state resources at its disposal, and also had the unconditional support of national and foreign accomplices, to mold the country into one that reflected the exact ideology that the Castros desired. These accomplices around the globe still disgustingly copy and repeat the views formulated and concocted in the laboratories of the Communist Party.

Castro has cultivated a powerful propaganda arsenal, both at home and abroad, which is strengthened with the elimination of the freedom of the press. This began in the early months of the guerillas' arrival in Havana. The regime's propaganda experts sold an image in which Cuba was a non-progressive, failing nation, whose geography was ravaged by capitalist exploitation and urgently needed the intervention of a savior. This "savior" was cast as a legitimate revolutionary who would save the Cuban people from this nightmare.

This "redeemer" and his cohorts indeed arrived one morning in January 1959 and helped end the seven-year dictatorship of General Fulgencio Batista y Zaldivar.

However, it was only to impose another dictatorship, which has lasted more than half a century. This rebellion was wrongfully portrayed as one of romantic and heroic valor. In reality, they froze the development of the nation, shut down its economic growth, and set in motion one of the key elements necessary for totalitarianism: economic misery and disparity.

The real depiction of Cuba, where Leopoldo Fernández Pujals lived until he was 13 years old, became a state secret. It was a forbidden testimony because it uncovered the truth and the scheme of precariousness and disaster of the communists' false narrative. The country's history, its continuous progress, economic stability, daring entrepreneurs and successful businessmen became part of a past considered shameful by the new hierarchy. They confiscated everything from large industries in full production to the nation's bountiful farms and private individuals' homes, cars, jewelry, and wardrobes.

The barrage of the propaganda highlighting the great political and military battles, the portrayal of progress and happiness for workers and their families – lies, lies, and more lies – completely eclipsed Cuba's true past, present, and future. All the deceptions left the real data buried forever, such as Cuba's impressive gold and U.S. dollar reserve of $373 million in 1958, ranked third in Latin America. The average Cuban of the last four generations never knew, and probably still does not know, that the country's annual gross national income was $2.34 billion and $520 per capita at that time.

It is a silent and buried fact that the nation, once the largest sugar producer in the world in the late '50s, with 163 sugar mills distributed throughout six provinces, 33,384 factories and 65,872 commercial enterprises, now needs to import sugar. Today, there are only 46 mills to grind the very scant sugar cane. Even this small amount of cane is on the verge of disappearing, because of the marabou weed, a thorny bush with a strong root system that is taking over fertile land abandoned by the idle and unproductive communist cooperatives, which were formed by seizing and "nationalizing" farms. That is to say, stealing them away from rightful owners.

The 6 million citizens residing on the island of Cuba during the pre-Castro era were not forced to enthusiastically and gratefully applaud daily watered-down information about the revolutionary medical system. Unfortunately, citizens today are. Back in the '50s, Cubans were not forced to read communist propaganda from the country's only newspaper. Over five decades ago, there were 58 newspapers, 126 weeklies and 160 radio stations, so Cubans knew that their country had the lowest infant mortality rate and the highest number of hospital beds per inhabitant in the region. Cuba was ranked 22nd globally in terms of doctors per patient, ranking it alongside the biggest free market nations in the world.

The children of Cuba during pre-Castro times were not forced to attend classes in centers of indoctrination, where, before learning basic math, they must learn to raise their hand every morning to make a military salute and say, "We will be like Che." Today, children are.

In that pre-Castro nation, there were almost 2,000 kindergartens and 8,900 elementary schools, where, every Friday, the Cuban flag was waved and the national anthem sung. There were 1,700 private schools, 240 of higher education, 171 institutes and numerous academies of commerce, technology, agriculture, forestry, arts, surveying and journalism. There were three public and nine private universities.

Cuba went from being a poor but emerging country to a wretched territory starved and obsessed in everyday life with what is called, with the Caribbean sense of humor, the two serious day-to-day issues: lunch and dinner. The notion of a ration card did not exist before Castro. Certainly there were very poor and disadvantaged people in society, but studies by independent experts and highly respected institutions have found that meat consumption per person per year was 76 pounds, with another 12 pounds of chicken, 47 eggs, and a total of 2,800 calories a day per individual.

In the summer of 1963 the totalitarian regime implemented the so-called ration card, a sinister control document for staple foods. That infamous card is still in effect today and recently celebrated a half-century of existence.

Beef, seafood, and quality fish and chicken disappeared from the dining room tables of the Cuban family. Rice, beans, vegetables, potatoes, and fruits suddenly became luxury items. Yet, even as those proteins are beginning to reappear due to the regime relaxing control over the private sector, these foods are sold at such high prices that the Cuban people, with an average salary of $20 per month, cannot afford them. Children may receive a milk allowance, but only until they are 7 years old. When Raúl Castro replaced his brother in power, he guaranteed a daily glass of milk for every citizen. They are still waiting for it, for their breakfast!

Convinced that it is impossible to achieve economic productivity under socialism, the regime begins to awkwardly and slowly return to a state capitalism of snacks and lemonade. It lets Cubans open small shops to sell bread and soft drinks and authorizes the opening of restaurants, bars, and small private businesses, usually funded with money from Cubans who have emigrated and whose relatives stayed on the island. More seriously, the military dictatorship is starting a handover process of businesses and enterprises, snatched from their rightful owners, to foreign investors.

To promote foreign investment in Cuba, a new law was implemented that offers easy access and guarantees to businessmen of the European Union, Mexico,

Brazil, and other countries to invest in Cuba. These facilities are in a free zone in the port of Mariel and in major commercial areas, like the mythical Manzana de Gómez in the center of the capital which was the property of a famous Cuban family. After five decades of neglect, the ownership of the building has been transferred to discreet but ambitious Swiss businessmen.

The main issue is that regular Cuban citizens operate in the limited universe of their commercial cubbyholes, while foreigners invest large sums of money in the island. The end result is that the group of cronies in power, and their descendants, continue partying and living their lavish lifestyle in the palace of the revolution.

The consequence of imposing socialism on the people of the island was that individual and political freedom and the economic progress of Cuba was halted as if it had its roots cut off by a machete. The regime persecuted the private initiative and imprisoned those who tried to make a living outside the clutches of the totalitarian state.

Leopoldo Fernández Pujals' family, Cubans with a tradition and history of being entrepreneurs, patriots and independent professionals, were, without knowing it, natural enemies of the new dictators. His ancestors worked closely with José Martí to fight Spanish colonialism and later set up prosperous businesses in the republic. Some of his close relatives fought the Batista dictatorship. His parents were professionals unconcerned with the political arena in the country and were entirely devoted to their professions and family.

A decent and democratic Cuba was the ideal for young Leopoldo, who wanted to be an agricultural engineer and have his own business, to develop his talent. When things began to blur in Havana in 1960, the family decided they should leave Cuba for a while and return when the waters had retreated. Yet, over time, the water rose higher and higher, and, therefore, Leopoldo and his family stayed in United States and had to start a new life from scratch.

His story is complete in this autobiography and what we must do now is a little reflection about how totalitarianism and all its variants disguised as democratic ruses, like *"chavismo,"* ruin countries and close the space to those who generate wealth, progress, and prosperity with their own effort, tenacity, and tireless work.

The author of this book learned on his own and trained himself as an entrepreneur in the United States. He founded his companies, succeeded in his businesses, and is well known in Spain. Nevertheless, the imposition of an ideology and the power of a military dictatorship did not allow him the privilege of achieving his goals in the land that he loves. This also deprived Cuba, a ghost of the one he dreamed of, of having him among its citizens that would have helped it become a better country.

This book contains the thrill of a life, or, rather, many lives. Additionally, it serves as a teaching tool for young aspiring entrepreneurs on the one hand, and for people prone to discouragement and defeat on the other. It is also a warning for those looking for magic formulas in a dilapidated communist ideology and its rags to solve eventual mistakes and bumps that we experience in democratic nations.

I think that Mr. Fernández Pujals makes a quiet and warm recognition of the Leopoldos who remained vanquished, imprisoned, or with their dreams crumbled in Cuba. It is also a warning to those that might arise in nations that fall under any of the different variants of totalitarian dictatorships and their false saviors posing as champions of the poor.

Raúl Ramón Rivero Castañeda is a poet, journalist, and Cuban dissident.

How My Children Remember Me

ALEJANDRO CENTURIÓN
45 years old, a neurologist practicing in the United States.

I have learned a lot from my father and have admired him since I was a child. During my infancy, he instilled principles in me, including the importance of working hard and the fulfillment of responsibilities. He taught me that you must be demanding with yourself, find discipline in your daily life in order to become a better person and achieve your goals. He often said that you have to work to earn what you deserve, that things in life are not free, and that money does not grow on trees.

My father has a very strict work ethic and is very disciplined. When I was a little older he talked about having dreams and asserted that anything could be achieved if one works hard and is persistent. He also inculcated in me the importance of values like loyalty and honesty. One of the teachings that has remained in my memory is to be positive in the face of any difficulty. Another value that he has taught me is to appreciate liberty and the importance of human rights. Since my father was born in Cuba and lost everything, those values are very important to him. When I was graduating from college, he was creating the Elena Mederos Foundation: First Human Rights, to disseminate information about the violations of these rights in Cuba and to help bring freedom back to the Cuban people. In recent years I have been personally involved in raising awareness about human rights violations by the communist regime in China.

In the professional field, my father is an entrepreneur and a born leader. He is very creative, always thinking of new ideas. When he has a goal, he is persistent until he achieves success.

On a personal level, although he is a winner who strives for perfection, he is a very simple person who is just as happy eating canned food as he is dining in an upscale restaurant. Even though he is accustomed to today's comforts, he appreciates and enjoys the simple things in life, like spending time with his family.

My father is also involved in a number of philanthropic causes. Among his future goals is that we, his children, achieve our goals and dreams in life. He already has achieved his main dream, to have his own business, and is now undertaking others, including improving the PRE breed of Spanish Horse, something that produces a lot of enthusiasm and will help him to continue enjoying life in the future as he ages gracefully.

CARLOS CENTURIÓN
38 years old, entrepreneur and owner of two growing restaurant chains.

The first images I have of my father have to do with how much he worked while employed at Johnson & Johnson in Spain. He taught me one must start from the bottom and I remember that he put me to work in the central supply warehouse at TelePizza in Valdemoro. Even though I was not of legal age to do so, he wanted me to find out how much and how hard you have to work to earn money and that to really know how to run a business, you have to start from the bottom.

Another thing that I remember about him is that he let us choose the career we wanted to pursue. My eldest brother wanted to be a pediatrician. My father, thanks to his contacts at Johnson & Johnson, arranged for my brother to accompany the chief of pediatric surgery at 12th de Octubre Hospital in Madrid. After that summer, my brother decided that he did not want to be a surgeon and ended up specializing in neurology. I wanted to be a dentist and after working for two weeks with my father's dentist, I was convinced that the profession was not as attractive as I had thought. Afterward, during my college years, I decided to concentrate on the restaurant trade.

What surprised me the most was his financial support, which allowed me to be the sole owner of a restaurant. Although I told him that I was not ready, he convinced me that "You only learn to castrate by removing the testicles." It was a wise decision, because in the last six years I have learned and grown. I now feel ready to open more restaurants and have a restaurant business as big as TelePizza.

ALBERTO FERNÁNDEZ
23 years old, recent college graduate and owner of a music event business in the United States

The most important lesson I have learned from my father is to develop the right habits. He has taught me two things. By having good habits you have the power to find happiness and success, and bad habits can take control of you and prevent you from being successful. I have seen my father put into action the lessons he has learned, because he is constantly trying to implement good habits while getting rid of bad ones.

Two of the most difficult moments that my parents had to go through was when my father was fired from the company he had founded, TelePizza, and when my brother Andrés had a liver transplant. Both of these things happened while I was too little to fully understand what was going on. While growing up and having a better understanding of what had happened, I realized that my mother and my father had the strength, optimism, and patience to overcome these extremely difficult situations. I think that most people would have thrown in the towel.

I hope to continue enjoying my father's company in the future, because I still have a lot to learn from his knowledge, experience, and metaphors.

ANDRÉS FERNÁNDEZ
21 years old, third-year college student in the United States

My father is constantly teaching me something new, but there are two lessons that I will never forget. The first one was on the golf course when I was younger, which is that constant practice leads to perfection. The second lesson is about how to be a better person, by substituting bad habits with good and constructive ones.

I could define my father in one word: autodidactic. The mentality of a self-taught person is when confronted with a problem they look for a solution; they execute a plan and analyze the results. Then they make changes to the plan if necessary and repeat the process until it is perfect. It is what he calls "the management cycle." My father believes that everyone can be self-reliant, and can overcome *excusitis*, or inflammation of the excuse if they go to bed every day after following the management cycle.

One of my father's common phrases, and my personal favorite, is "no comas mierda." Literally, in English, this translates to: "Do not eat shit." Metaphorically, it means doing something that is not constructive or something that does not help a person meet their goals in life. I heard this phrase many times during my adolescence. When I was playing video games my father would come into my bedroom and ask me, *"Estas comiendo mierda?"*

Now that I am attending a university, every time I am playing too many video games or doing something that does not help me reach my goals, I can hear his voice in my head asking me, *"Estas comiendo mierda?* Are you eating shit?"* I laugh a little and immediately leave the remote control on the floor in order to go and do something productive.

ALFONSO FERNÁNDEZ
20 years old, beginning college student in the United States

Children learn from parents, or whoever is the authority figure in the household. I have been fortunate to have a father who was very much involved when I was very young, teaching me good manners. I did not understand it at the time and, in some cases, I rebelled. However, over the years I have come to appreciate what he taught me. When I was in boarding school in the United States, I witnessed improper behavior at the dinner table that made quite an impression on me. Since then I valued the education that my parents had given me, and I have felt very privileged.

I remember when I started to participate in soccer, a sport requiring a lot of training, I practiced running and eventually I became captain of the team. Two qualities stood out in my behavior in relation to my teammates: how much I trained after hours in my free time and that I never complained. The no-complaining behavior I owe to my father, but I also learned from him to be productive, think positively, respect everybody, and always be humble, along with a long list of other things.

ANECDOTES OF LEOPOLDO FERNÁNDEZ PUJALS
Compiled by Pedro Español

I remember one occasion where we had to launch a TV advertising campaign for the Centurion PRE horse farm, for which he had allocated a budget of 300,000 euros. I mentioned this to my mother, and she said, "Sonia, you must have misunderstood, because it is impossible to have that kind of money in your hands when you have no idea of marketing!" But it was true. He put challenges in front of his employees until he got the results he wanted.

SONIA VÍLCHEZ

It had never happened before that a Cuban multi-millionaire, who was extremely successful, met with former political prisoners and promised that he would provide the financial support to us, the *Plantados*. With the passage of time I was able to confirm that his backing went beyond what we could have imagined, and that he was not only our sponsor but another *Plantado*, another immovable friend. During the initial months, when all five of us traveled and gave speeches promoting freedom in Cuba, we sort of represented some type of collective Mandellas. Leo would send us the necessary funding to cover our salaries and administrative and traveling expenses. Later on, he really surprised us. He sent us a million U.S. dollars. We could not believe it!

ÁNGEL DE FANA

In a golf tournament, in which Leo and I were partners, the organizers had given Leo a handicap that was six strokes above his official one. This error would have been beneficial to us. He called the administrator of the tournament to request that his handicap be lowered from 20 to 14. It was an important tournament that every participant wanted to win, not only for the notoriety but also for the prize money.

FERNANDO VEGA-PENICHET

I met Leo one month before the qualifying rounds to obtain the golf card to participate on the European tour. At the end of the meeting, he stated that if I were to get the European golf card, he would sponsor me. Thirty days later I got the European tour card and he kept his word. He provided me with a lot of money, 150,000 euros. After nine years, and having won seven tournaments on the European tour, he has been the best sponsor I have ever had.

Looking back, I now realize that Leo sponsored me when I was a "Mr. Nobody," without previously knowing me and without asking me for anything in return.

GONZALO FERNÁNDEZ-CASTAÑO

One day Leo told me that he had been fired from his own company. I reminded him of a phrase that my grandfather used to say: "You entrusted flowers to a donkey, and he ate them." Months later, he said he wanted me to become part of the Board of Directors of TelePizza. I replied that I could not visualize myself sitting around the table with such important people, where I thought I did not fit. He then told me that I was already on the approved list. A few days later, he organized a dinner for everybody to get to know each other. Everyone was introducing themselves, and when my turn came, I asked Leo, "How do I introduce myself? What can I say?" Leo reassured me, saying, "Do not worry, I will introduce you," and then he said, "I have chosen Ángel, because when none of us knows what to do, we will ask Ángel what his wise grandfather would have said, and that is what we will do."

ÁNGEL LOZANO

Leo was not afraid of correcting employees, no matter what. When a female employee came to work inadequately and unprofessionally dressed, we were incapable of addressing the issue. However, Leo was not shy and he dared to do what other managers were afraid to do. On one occasion, he even went as far as to send an employee home to change into proper office attire.

CARLOS GÓMEZ

186

He had the ability to stretch the rope and then loosen it up before it snapped. When he achieved his goals, he would know how to squeeze just a little bit more out of you. One time we went to buy a number of magic tricks in Hong Kong. They offered every trick for 100 pesetas. Leo thought it was outrageous and offered 30 pesetas. The Chinese vendor accepted and we shook hands. Leo turned around and said to me quietly, "Carlos, I cannot believe it. I think we have negotiated poorly. We could have gotten the tricks for a lot lower price."

CARLOS GÓMEZ

When Leo explained his theory of the inverted pyramid, he said we had to always be "facing the customer with our backs to our superiors." It is a phrase that, if it were correctly understood by everyone, would lead to success in any enterprise.

CARLOS GRAY

Leo was capable of convincing you the idea that "white" was the best and that we had to promote it as our priority. All of us would buy into this, and "white" became our priority. For whatever reason, he was capable, a few days later, of telling us that what was "white" before now was "red" and that "red" was now the best. He was such a good salesman that you would walk out of his office believing that what was "white" was "red" now, that red was the best, and whole-heartedly promoting "red."

JOSÉ MANUEL ESCRIBAÑO

At a shareholders meeting in London, a small group of investors who came from Madrid protested, disrupted the meeting, and they even insulted the board members. Leo immediately stood up and firmly stated that not only was he investing a large part of his net worth into Jazztel, but that he was also convinced that the business plan would be successful. I could not believe how quickly Leo appeased them, to the point that they even asked him forgiveness for their behavior. The turmoil ended in a nearby pub, with everyone drinking beer and having their photographs taken with Leo.

JOSÉ MIGUEL GARCÍA

I remember going to Oropesa in Toledo for an Easter vacation. It was Saturday evening and I got a phone call from Leo, who was at the temporary headquarters in the pizzeria in Santa María de la Cabeza. Leo informed me that the computers were down. As quickly as I could, I drove my car directly to the store. When I arrived I found that the only problem was that the printer was out of paper. I could not believe it! I said, "Leo, I have come all the way from Oropesa and the only problem is that the printer is out of paper!" He replied, "The printer is out of paper...and you are in Oropesa?"

JUAN CARLOS GARCIA

I was having a difficult time in my life after going through my second cancer operation. There were rumors that there would be many job dismissals after Leo returned to the Presidency of TelePizza. My colleague and I were convinced that we were going to be fired. Leo called us into his office, staring straight into our eyes, something that he taught us to do, and told us, "Last night, before I went home, I had given instructions for the two of you to be fired this morning. However, I have thought overnight that if the two of you wish to continue working at TelePizza with enthusiasm, you can remain on the payroll." We both said yes, and he said to us: "So nothing has happened here." Before we left his office, Leo inquired about my health, which touched my soul. I will never forget that moment.

LUISA RODRIGUEZ

Leo only has the signs of addition (+) and multiplication (x) in his mental calculations. He does not use the rest of the signs. He is the man of exponential equations.

MIGUEL ÁNGEL RODRIGUEZ

At a press conference after Leo's investment in Jazztel had been announced, a journalist asked, "Well, Mr. Fernández, you have now invested, but when are you selling? Are you speculating? And then what?" Leo replied, "I think that is a question in very poor taste. It is as if I am going to your wedding and asking you, 'After marrying your wife, when will you announce your divorce?'" The journalist was left dumbfounded as everybody burst out laughing.

RAMÓN QUINTERO

I remember during the 1993 economic slowdown, we defined the job description of the direct marketing specialist (DMS). There were executives who were very pessimistic, and some were saying that we had peaked and that we should stop opening new stores. When Leo heard that, he said, "We have peaked?" He decided to go and work full time alongside the manager of the store on Santa María de la Cabeza Street. There, on trial, was the new position of the DMS. In less than six months he more than doubled the sales of that store. His decision to work at that store motivated all the executives of the company to get rid of their *Office-itis* and to follow his lead. The sales throughout the company began to grow substantially.

RICARDO GARRASTAZU

One time I was having a drink with coworkers and I began to imitate his Cuban accent. Suddenly, all of my coworkers' faces changed. I suspected Leo had entered the room. I was afraid I was going to be fired; nevertheless he came near me, gave me a pat on the back, and said, "Continue, continue, you are doing very well." It amused me to imitate him, and all of his famous phrases: "What does not grow dies," or "One must distinguish between what is vital, what is important, and what is secondary." I thought if you were learning the four or five key phrases you could become an entrepreneur. It seemed easy.

RICARDO GARRASTAZU

One day Leo said to me, "You could be a great entrepreneur, but you will not, because you are not strong enough. You must be firm to be an entrepreneur." Leo has always been firm but fair.

RICARDO GARRASTAZU

When we were filming the first TelePizza TV commercial, Leo showed up at the studio set unannounced. We were all very nervous because we wanted to ensure that it went well. We asked him if he wanted a drink and, very quietly, he requested some ham and a glass of wine. His demeanor made us all feel relaxed.

RICARDO GARRASTAZU

Leo suggested that I become involved in the purchasing of mares and stallions for the Centurion PRE Horse Farm. I told him that I did not have any experience in that field and that most likely I would be taken advantage of. I will never forget his response: "Go and buy horses, son, and do not worry, because we will learn from your mistakes." A little later, I was selling horses and raised doubts about how to treat customers when they wanted to buy a horse. He did not think twice and replied, "Treat them as you would like them to treat you."

RICHI MOUTOUSS

I had been working for six months at the first store, Pizza Phone. Leo asked me if I was interested in continuing to work at Pizza Phone. He caught me by surprise. "What do you mean? At this pizza store?" Then Leo said, "No, no, no, I plan to open 200 stores like this one." I thought he was crazy and that he was exaggerating. Yet he explained to me how this was going to be achieved. I decided to discontinue my university studies and started working full time to make a career in the business.

PEDRO RIVAS

The TelePizza IPO at the Madrid Stock Exchange was a spectacular event. I thoroughly enjoyed accompanying Leo as he entered the trading floor. Everyone there wore a suit and a tie, and I was there with my TelePizza uniform. We spent a couple of hours giving our pizza slices to everyone present. I remember Leo giving me a hug and saying, "Juanba, TelePizza's shares are now being traded on the Madrid Stock Exchange!"

JUAN BAUTISTA GALÁN

We flew to Poland to participate in the opening of the first TelePizza store in that country. I decided to take a suit and tie, thinking that we should be dressed elegantly. When Leo saw me dressed that way, he asked, "Where do you think you are going, to a wedding?" I quickly understood the message and took off my jacket and tie and never again dressed that way working for the company.

JOSE MERODIO

During the sale of some of Leo's TelePizza shares, I went to the bank to renegotiate downward a commission of 24 million pesetas. I was happy when I got it reduced to 500,000. The surprise to me was when I went to inform Leo, he replied very seriously that the deal would not be done because he had a verbal agreement with the bank, BBVA, that there would be zero commission. That night I did not sleep. The next day, I went to the branch of the bank to explain what had happened, and they could not believe it. Finally, this transaction closed without any commissions, and I learned that the most important thing that counts is your word.

FERNANDO BENAVENTE

My husband, Alan, and I met Leo and Marilina at a Spanish PRE horse show in the United States. We invited them to stay at our home in Wyoming. We never thought they would come, because most people say they would like to but never actually do. To our surprise, they came with their three young children, and in five days we drove over a thousand miles and enjoyed staying at Yellowstone National Park. Leo had kept his word.

CELIA STENFORS-DACRE

At a restaurant in Miami Lakes, sitting at the bar, Leo started a conversation with a Caterpillar salesman. After the usual small talk, the crane salesman asked Leo, "What do you do?" Leo told him, "I sell pizzas."

MAURICIO CLAVER-CARONE

The day I turned 50 years old, Leo showed up at my birthday party with one of the employees from his farm. They had brought me a gift. It was nothing less than a horse. Although I love these animals, I must admit that I wondered, "Now what will I do with this horse in my home?"

ANTONIO CATALÁN

Leo liked to eat at a local ribs restaurant that offered gift coupons for future purchases, which he saved. Once you had saved a number of coupons, you could get a free meal. Who would imagine that of a wealthy person? Then I realized that he enjoyed participating in the local restaurant discount program.

JOSÉ ORTIZ

Leo said, "Look, José Manuel, I do not wish to be an old man, and before closing my eyes for the last time, having to say 'But why did I not do it?' What the hell, I will do it. I will do it now."

JOSÉ MANUEL ESCRIBANO

When one of the senior managers at Johnson & Johnson in Spain said that he was leaving the company to work with Leo at TelePizza because he had been offered 5 percent of the shares of the company, we not only thought that Leo was crazy but that the executive was even crazier. We thought that the 5 percent would never be worth more than what the executive was collecting from his annual salary. In a few years, we realized that we were all wrong.

CARLOS GÓMEZ

One afternoon I went to see Leo at the pizzeria, and as always, he was with his small but famous musical calculator. When he saw me, he said enthusiastically, "we have the biggest pizza restaurant in Madrid, with the most tables. Fifty thousand homes, fifty thousand tables. Who has something similar?"

JOSÉ MANUEL ESCRIBANO

One day, Leo said, "son, you are going to offer me the best cheese price on the market, because I can assure that in two years, we will be bigger than Pizza Hut and Domino's in Spain." I thought, "this guy is either nuts or is enlightened." However, I did not have much to lose, and I accepted because he sold the idea with such logic that it made me think he could accomplish it.

LUIS CARLOS PALACIOS

From Leo I learned to appreciate just about everything, including very small details, like saving money by switching off a light or turning off water tap when it was not necessary to have it running.

PEDRO RIVAS

We saw Leo hundreds of times putting his hands in the tomato bucket when he was preparing the tomato sauce. He used to say, "in our veins we have tomato sauce instead of blood."

EDUARDO ARMIJO

I vividly remember how upset my parents were when I informed them that I was going to begin working full time at the pizza store. Evidently my parents did not understand how I could drop my studies to become a lawyer to work in a pizzeria. I had to leave my parents' home, because living there became unbearable. From that moment on, I followed his Vision.

EDUARDO ARMIJO

Every TelePizza top executive had a more expensive car than Leo, in spite of Leo being the President of the company. Leo reinvested absolutely everything back into the business.

JAVIER GISBERT

An employee of the Centurion PRE horse farm, when asked the name of a particular mare, was saying at random any name. This behavior continued until Leo one day told him, "You have given me the wrong name of that mare. The name you have just said has no white on any of her forelegs, and this one has two white hind legs." Unbelievably, Leo had memorized the names of the 300 mares, their sizes, color, and whether or not they had white legs. From that day on, that employee made an effort to learn all the names of the mares and to speak the truth.

ANA BALLESTEROS

As anyone might imagine Leo is smart and extraordinary, but what perhaps not everyone gets to experience is his humor and unique manner of approaching problems. From Leo I have learned the importance of making quick calculations, thinking big, and solving problems in one's sleep. He is fond of citing Confucius who said that a young man goes to sleep with a problem in his mind and awakens with an answer in hand. It is amazing what can be accomplished if you trust your dreams and stick to your principles.

MICHAEL MCALLISTER